"Ken Forkish's latest book is a masterwork. *Evolutions in Bread* offers an old-yet-new approach, focusing not on rustic European loaves but on comfort breads with a softer crumb, like brioche and milk bread. All can be made in a loaf pan or a Dutch oven, with or without a sourdough starter. Beautiful recipes! But I'd buy this book just for its transformative toast. Once you've tried that, the mere memory will bounce you happily out of bed in the morning."

—**DARRA GOLDSTEIN,**
founding editor of *Gastronomica* and author of
Beyond the North Wind* and *Fire + Ice

"Ken Forkish writes books that people use. In *Evolutions in Bread*, he brings us from farm to mill to hearth, and along this journey Alan Weiner's photos bring beauty in ways rarely seen when shooting dough and bread. It's been ten years since Ken's legendary *Flour Water Salt Yeast* and we should all be ready to follow this evolution as outlined by one of the truly great teachers."

—**STEPHEN JONES, founder of WSU Breadlab**

"As a home baker who has spent many hours with Ken Forkish's books, *Evolutions in Bread* is a new best! He shares his new—even simpler—starter method, easy-to-follow recipes, and plenty of tricks and secrets to create the most incredible bread—all from your own kitchen!"

—**ABBY WAMBACH, Olympian, activist, and**
#1 *New York Times* bestselling author of *Wolfpack*

"A wonderfully in-depth look at what is possible at home with the right teacher. Ken shows us endless ways to explore the many wonders of pan breads, utilizing heirloom wheats and sharing his passion for low-waste techniques. This book gave me the courage to jump back into baking at home and I'm sure it will do the same for you."

—**SEAN BROCK, chef and owner of**
Audrey and June

"*Evolutions in Bread* takes the artisanal love of bread baking to the next level. This book has so much information and explains it in such simple detail that anyone passionate about producing a great loaf can master many different styles. I, being a bread nerd, am obsessed!"

—**KEN ORINGER, James Beard Award–winning**
chef and restaurateur

"Ken's first book, *Flour Water Salt Yeast*, became an instant classic in the world of artisan bread books, making his craft accessible to home bakers and professionals as well. Ken's method for sourdough in *Evolutions in Bread* has evolved to make it more user-friendly, and all the recipes here were tested in regular home ovens, which can be temperamental, especially for bakers. In your hands you have the roadmap to making excellent bread in your own kitchen."

—**FRANCISCO MIGOYA, head chef of**
Modernist Cuisine

EVOLUTIONS IN BREAD

EVOLUTIONS IN BREAD

Artisan Pan Breads and Dutch-Oven Loaves at Home

KEN FORKISH

James Beard Award–winning author of *Flour Water Salt Yeast*

Photographs by Alan Weiner

TEN SPEED PRESS

California | New York

CONTENTS

INTRODUCTION

Time flies. As I write this, a decade has passed since *Flour Water Salt Yeast* was first published in 2012. That book helped home bakers craft round, crusty Dutch-oven loaves of a similar quality to what you can find at a very good artisan bakery. I explained the methods that we use at my bakery in Portland, Oregon, and I adapted them for use in home kitchens. First-time home bakers using *Flour Water Salt Yeast* routinely shared triumphant photos of the bread coming out of their own ovens. The book has many solid foundational recipes, an instructional chapter that explains the details that go into making artisan bread at home (e.g., think of time and temperature as ingredients), and then a detailed essay titled "Making a Bread (or Pizza) Dough You Can Call Your Own." The versatility of *Flour Water Salt Yeast* is in the template that each recipe provides; use whatever blend of flour you want. I figured that was it, you had all the tools now, nothing more for me to say. I didn't think I had a future bread book in me.

Times change! We make a bread at Ken's Artisan Bakery called pain rustique. Unlike our rustic country breads, the pain rustique is a soft sandwich and toast bread made from our baguette dough. It's popular, and too often when I've wanted to grab one to take home, we've been sold out or nearly so; I'm not going to take the last loaf. It's a little weird to own a bakery and then go home and bake a loaf for myself, but that's what I started doing, and that's when my pan-loaf mission took over. These pan-loaf breads ended up nothing like the crusty levain breads, baguettes, or ciabatta we make at the bakery. But they gave me what I wanted from the pain rustique loaves: a bread that had

the goodness of a long-fermented dough; a little retro (I like the comfort of it); and designed for sandwiches, toast, croutons, tapas, stale-bread dog snacks, and pizza toast. These old-style pan breads became a new normal in my house—at first a step away from more rustic Dutch-oven loaves and then, a few loaves later, a happy choice. Same dough. Which style of loaf to bake? This was flexibility beyond the recipes in my first book, and it inspired me to create new doughs as well. The recipes in this book—all new—mostly give you a choice of baking the same dough into a pan loaf or a Dutch-oven loaf.

Loaves like those that I started baking at home—artisan pan breads—haven't received much attention in the cookbook world. In many bakeries that I've admired in France—my original muses—it's very common to see pan loaves such as pain de mie, as well as others. I didn't invent artisan pan bread; rather, I just acknowledged my own joy in it, and I hope you do too. These loaves are often baked from a bubbly, wet, and sticky dough, so they sometimes look kind of funky. They can be made up from a simple straight dough or with a sourdough culture, and they can be ready from start to finish in about six hours. Or they can work on an overnight schedule and be ready to bake in the morning. They last for five days without going stale, the flavor is far better than a supermarket sliced bread, and the ingredients list is far shorter. The texture when slices are toasted is sublime—crisp and delicate on the outside, tender in the middle. Your morning toast will get a big upgrade. My dog, Junior, is a big fan.

It makes sense. Old-style, home-baked pan breads can be made using the elements that define good artisan baking—long fermentation, high-quality ingredients, sourdough cultures, and high-temp baking. It's not difficult. Wouldn't you love to make sandwich bread that's of the same quality as the rustic round loaves in *Flour Water Salt Yeast*? These pan loaves are my newest, and lasting, bread crush. As I was test-baking Dutch-oven loaves and ran out of pan bread, I quickly made a fresh one. Why is that? You'll see. My test bakers had the same takeaway—a new bread type that's at once familiar yet more delicious and more desirable than before. Friends of recipe testers asked, "What's the secret ingredient?" The same as before: flour, water, salt, and yeast. Time and technique. No surprises there.

During the tinkering process for the pan-bread recipes, I tried making up a Dutch-oven loaf from the same dough. It worked great; one recipe now produces two completely different breads. I was fully into the game at this stage, and my next step was to revise the process for the sourdough recipes from my first book and decrease the amount of waste (extra sourdough that you throw away). The result is a method to make up a new natural levain (sourdough) culture that calls for only a small fraction of the flour that the *Flour Water Salt Yeast* levain used. I also figured out a simplified, flour-efficient way to use this culture in these recipes. The levain in this book follows the example of my second book, *The Elements of Pizza*. But I adapted its use for bread baking, as bread and pizza doughs have different needs (bread dough requires a lot more rise). Once you establish your own sourdough (it's a cinch and takes a few minutes a day for a week), you keep it in the refrigerator. Pluck from it to make a new dough as needed and refresh it every seven to ten days. It's not required for most of these recipes, but it will make them better.

My favorite part of cookbook authoring is the developmental stages that I go through before writing begins. This entails many months of baking at home, testing concepts, refining, refiguring levain on a not-every-day baking schedule, and, in this case, wondering if I could make pan breads that are as desirable as the cool-looking round loaves that bake in a Dutch oven. I got jazzed making a New York–style rye with caraway seeds for a Reuben sandwich. Japanese milk bread is worth its hype, and I wanted to master that and present it to you so you can make your own. This book's brioche loaf is on a par with the one we've made at my bakery for twenty years. Then there are particular sourdough cultures with fruit, like one I used to make at Ken's Artisan that is hydrated with apple cider, and this book's apple bread is a faithful rendition. Dense rye bread made with a sourdough culture—that's in here too. And several recipes have fun stuff in the bread, like black rice flour, corn flour, or tea-soaked raisins and their liquid.

The old is new again! Einkorn, emmer, and spelt are varieties of wheat that date back to ancient times and the beginning of civilization. Yet flour from these grains was extremely hard to find even ten years ago. A growing number of farmers have been planting fields with these varieties and others that just taste better than wheat grown for the mass market. Some are as old as old gets, and there is an increasing market for them. You might hear the names *heritage grains*, *ancient wheat varieties*, and *landrace wheat* to describe these flours. Stone milling brings out the best in these grains, and the recent trend has been for wheat farmers and farm collectives to bring the milling in-house and then sell direct to bakers and consumers. It is progress that I've long wished for. Landrace varieties of wheat, like Rouge de Bordeaux, and modern hybrids, like Edison, shift the mind-set of wheat as solely a commodity product to wheat that has varietal characteristics just as apples,

cherries, and grapes do, not to mention the possibility of terroir. There are several recipes here to make pan loaves and Dutch-oven breads from some of these high-quality grains. Once you try them, it's hard to stop.

I found everything about making bread at home is easier in one-loaf batch sizes, using a 6-quart tub to mix the dough by hand—no mixer needed for most. The dough will rise in the same tub that you mix it in. Most of the reasons for one-loaf recipes are obvious: less to measure out; less dough to shape, manage, and bake. When it's less work, I'm inclined to do it more often, and I'm hoping that you will be too.

There you have it. *Evolutions in Bread* creates a new category for the home baker: artisan pan breads. It makes sourdough easier and flour efficient. It gives you flexibility to make two and sometimes three different breads from the same recipe, as open-pan loaves, lidded-pan loaves, and Dutch-oven loaves. Make your own Multigrain Bread or dive into some creative recipes, like Black Bread, Butter Bread, Hazelnut Bread, and Apple-Cider Levain Bread, that will add range to any home baker's repertoire. The recipes that use emmer and einkorn flour, two ancient wheat varieties, are a must try.

As always, happy baking!

PART I
GETTING STARTED

STONE MILLED
ANCIENT GRAIN

ORGANIC

Emmer Wheat
Flour

CAMAS COUNTRY

4lb./1.81Kg   34-501 061621

EINKORN
WHOLE GRAIN FLOUR

GRIST & TOLL

—AN URBAN FLOUR MILL—

LOS ANGELES

STONE MILL

Rouge
Hard
W

4.0lb/1.81 Kg

Four generations of
the lush, fertile sout
more than 60 years
land and are now a
movement to produ
it's food as close to
Camas Country Mill, 90472
www.camascountrymill.co

CHAPTER 1
INGREDIENTS & EQUIPMENT

Baking excellent bread at home is easy, once you've done it a few times, if you have good instructions, a few pieces of versatile kitchen gear, and, as always, good-quality ingredients. Readers of my first book should review this section as there is plenty of new information on flour and where to buy it as well as bread pans to work with the recipes.

Ingredients

What kind of flour should you buy to make good bread at home? There are more choices than ever before if you are willing to buy online and seek out flour mills in your region. High-quality stone-milled flour is an option alongside the workhorse white flour that you can obtain at the store. Even the flour that I buy for my bakery is superior to what was available twenty years ago. Well-known bakers are promoting wheat farmers and craft mills like never before, and greater public demand is creating new markets for excellent flours and grains that you can bake with at home.

Some of the stories of interesting wheat varieties follow in this chapter, and there is more detail about heritage-grain flours in the recipe headnotes. I like white bread, too, and white bread flour has a strong supporting role in most of my craft-flour bread recipes, as I blend flours together to get a good rise and texture.

Flour, ancient grains, and additional varieties of wheat get the lion's share of this section, but let's first review the other ingredients: water, salt, and yeast. They all matter.

Water

Tap water is normally fine. Filtered tap water is probably better, depending on your source. If your water is good enough to drink, it's good enough for baking.

Salt

When baking, I prefer fine sea salt. Avoid iodized salt because iodine inhibits fermentation and you can taste it. Since the grain size of salt varies from source to source, volume measurements tend to be inconsistent. Therefore, it's far better to weigh your salt. I recommend using fine sea salt because it will dissolve quickly in the dough.

Salt slows the fermentation of bread dough, and that's a good thing. Without it, bread dough will rise very fast and taste insipid. Salt also somewhat inhibits water absorption by the flour, so it is often added at a second mix stage. The standard amount of salt in bread recipes is 2 percent of the weight of the flour. The generally accepted range is between 1.8 and 2.2 percent.

Yeast

All the recipes in this book except the Dutch-oven levain breads call for instant dried yeast. You're likely to find two or three kinds of yeast at the store: active dry, rapid rise, and instant. All these yeasts are the same species: *Saccharomyces cerevisiae*. What differentiates them is their coating, the way the yeast is manufactured, and performance. The rise times may vary a little bit from brand to brand, so pay attention to the recipe guidelines for volume expansion in the dough to tell you when to go on to the next step. At my bakery, we use Saf-Instant Red Yeast. I recommend that you buy a 16-ounce package of this yeast, which is available online. It will keep for a year if stored airtight in the refrigerator.

In my recipes, it isn't necessary to dissolve the dried yeast first. These doughs have a lot of water in them, so the yeast dissolves rapidly in the dough. Just sprinkle it on top and incorporate as you mix with a wet hand.

Professional bakers use the term *commercial yeast* to refer to what consumers think of as store-bought yeast. Commercial yeast is a monoculture, a single species of yeast (the aforementioned

WHEAT BERRY (KERNEL)

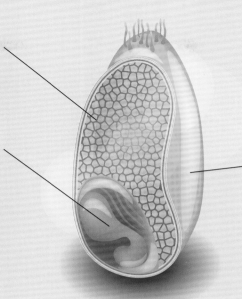

Endosperm
This is where white flour comes from. It is made up of starch and proteins and comprises about 84 percent of the wheat berry.

Germ
The component of the kernel that contains the wheat's genetic material; the germ makes up about 3 percent of the weight of the kernel. It contains all the fat and nutrients for the growth of the germ into a new plant if the seed were to be planted to grow wheat. It tastes good too.

Bran
Making up about 13 percent of the weight of the wheat berry, bran is the outer layer of the kernel; it surrounds and protects the endosperm and germ. Bran contains most of the dietary fiber of whole-wheat flour and most of the mineral content of the kernel.

S. cerevisiae). Levain cultures, in contrast, are made up of a community of yeasts that occur naturally in the flour and the environment, including the air. These wild yeasts aren't like commercial yeast; they are less vigorous and they impart their own particular flavors to the bread. Part of the complexity of flavors in a levain bread is due to multiple strains of yeast coexisting within the culture that is leavening the dough.

Commercial yeast causes bread dough to rise faster and provides more lift, producing bread with a lighter texture and more volume than levain breads. The slower yeast activity in levain dough allows time for naturally occurring lactic acid bacteria to undergo their own fermentation and impart acidity, which gives the bread more complex flavor, a bit of tang, and a heartier crust. And because of this acidity, levain breads keep longer before going stale.

Flour

As I wrote this, I was eating a piece of warm crust that flopped over the pan while my overproofed loaf of 50% einkorn pan bread was baking. Underneath the crunch was a deep, nutty wheat flavor that also had a nice tingle of acidity. I like many white breads, but they don't give me the rich flavor complexity that breads made with a craft-mill flour do. Still, the workhorse flour in my kitchen is a very-good-quality white bread flour. Even with my emmer or einkorn pan bread (which uses varieties of wheat that have been in existence for thousands of years), I blend an equal amount of white bread flour into the dough. The white bread flour has a protein quality that allows for good gluten formation and gives your bread more rise and a lighter texture. You still get the flavor and nutrition of the emmer or einkorn.

To understand flour, let's break down the components of the wheat berry and briefly review how milling works. Knowing these things will help guide your decisions on what flour to buy.

MILLING

Wheat crops are harvested and then threshed to separate the wheat berries from the head of the plant and the chaff so the berries are clean and ready for milling. Milling crushes the wheat berries and grinds them into flour.

Roller milling: This modern process, invented in the 1800s, has been the dominant milling method for industrial flour production worldwide since the early twentieth century. Roller milling has many manufacturing benefits; it allows for high volume, fast processing, and consistent quality production. Today's roller mills use stainless-steel tubes spaced very closely together to crush the wheat berries, and the process separates the germ and the bran from the white flour into three separate streams. Any packaging of whole-wheat flour from a roller mill is reconstituted, meaning that portions of bran and milled wheat germ are blended back in with white flour at a later point in the process. Ultimately, milling this way yields an affordable, dependable product that is far less expensive than is possible with traditional stone milling.

Stone milling: Milling stones can weigh thousands of pounds and are finely engineered and maintained to crush and grind wheat and other grains to very specific degrees of coarseness or fineness. Whole-grain flour from a stone mill means exactly that—all the grain that runs through the mill goes into the bag of flour at the end of the process. Sometimes the flour is sifted through bolting screens to separate out the bran, which leaves behind the ground endosperm and germ of the wheat berries. While stone milling was once the only method for grinding grains to make flour, in our modern times it is used only in smaller-scale operations; often to make heritage- and ancient-grain flour. The stone mill produces true whole-grain flours as

compared to the reconstituted whole-grain flour from roller mills. The germ of the wheat berry is crushed in stone mills and the flavors and oils of the germ are fully blended into the flour. There is some variability from one supplier of stone-milled flour to the next, and it's good to try from multiple sources to see what works best for you. At Ken's Artisan Bakery, we combine flour from stone mills with white flour from roller mills to create a blend that we think of as the best of both worlds to get optimal flavor, excellent texture, and consistent performance—and I do the same in many of this book's recipes.

HOW TO CHOOSE FLOUR

If I need to name-drop something that's available nationwide, I still recommend King Arthur flours. It is probably the best-quality flour brand available in stores. King Arthur offers a broad range of flours, and they are consistently made. Camas Country Mill is based in Oregon, and I've been using its flour at my bakeries for many years. It's a recommended place to buy einkorn, emmer, spelt, Red Fife, Rouge de Bordeaux, and other awesome bread flours, and its stone milling is of a superior quality compared with some others I've tested.

Online purchasing may be the best way to source one of the heritage-grain flours that I recommend in this book, and buying direct is how to do it, as most small mills are not sold on the big-box online shops. Filling orders from around the country is also an important way for a small craft mill to make ends meet. Good sources include Grist & Toll, Bluebird Grain Farms, Barton Springs Mill, Bench View Farms, Capay Mills, Anson Mills, Janie's Mill, and more. You may be getting flour that was milled within the week it shipped. Try it once and see the difference for yourself.

White Flour

White flour, made from the endosperm of the wheat berry, is really a wide selection of products to suit different applications, ranging from low-protein cake and pastry flours to high-protein bread flour. Wheat comes in thousands of varieties, primarily due to the work of plant breeders, and wheat-growing regions have climates and soil types that suit crops that were bred to work in that place. Protein is one element that varies from one wheat strain to another, each with different characteristics for the baker. When purchasing white flour

for bread baking, the protein content matters a lot, and there's a great variety. Your safest bet is to buy white flour in bags labeled "bread flour," which is kind of a dumb catch-all description because "whole wheat" is bread flour too.

Anything labeled "bread flour" will have a high-enough protein content, probably in the 12.5 to 13 percent range, to give your dough a generous rise. The protein translates as gluten, and the gluten is the structure that keeps the fermentation gases (CO_2 and ethanol) inside the loaf as it expands. I especially recommend higher-protein bread flour in recipes that combine it with weak gluten flours, like rye, emmer, einkorn, and spelt. The bread flour compensates, and blending it is a way to get a good rise and light texture when using these other flavorful flours that just don't rise as well.

All-purpose white flour has a protein content in the 9 to 12 percent range, depending on the brand; that's very broad. I advise using white flour with a minimum 10.5 percent protein content for my recipes; that's the lowest end of the protein spectrum for making bread that rises well. But this information isn't usually on the bag! If your brand doesn't give the loaf as much rise as you were expecting, it might help to try a bag that's marked "bread flour" next time. It's good to try different brands to find which ones work best for you.

To be clear, all my recipes that call for white flour specify "white bread flour" to ensure you will get a good rise, but many all-purpose white flours will work.

White Bread

I was raised on white bread, and I still appreciate it. I enjoy baguettes and ciabatta from my bakery, as much now as I did twenty years ago, for their classic-ness, their texture and light open crumb, and because the fermentation flavors from the pre-ferments we use, biga or poolish, are more prominent without the stronger flavors from the whole-grain flours. Pain de mie and other white sandwich breads will always have a place in the baker's repertoire. These breads aren't the same when made from whole-grain flour. Japanese milk bread is fun, too, and has a legitimate spot in the range of white breads.

Whole-Wheat Flour

A bag of whole-wheat flour has all of the wheat berry's parts: the endosperm that makes up white flour, the ground-up wheat germ, and the ground-up wheat bran. It has more vitamins, minerals, and dietary fiber than white flour. Its flavor is fuller and nuttier, too, and bread made with it will be denser than an all-white-flour bread (the bran in whole-grain flour cuts through and breaks down some of the gluten in the dough; the reduced gluten network holds less gas as a result, making a more compact texture). I blend whole-grain flour with white flour for flavor and nutrition, as in this book's The Standard loaf (see page 81).

When you buy whole-wheat flour at the grocery store, chances are it was roller milled, a process that divides the wheat berry into its three distinct parts, so the bran, the germ, and the white flour come out in three separate streams. Roller milling has a final assembly step to reconstitute the whole grain by adding back to white flour measured amounts of bran flour and wheat germ flour, presumably in proportions that are close to the original composition of the grain. Actually, you could also say that about 83 percent of a bag of whole-wheat flour is white flour, while 14 percent is the bran and 3 percent is the germ. Your whole-wheat flour is mostly white flour. Chew on that!

If your flour was stone milled, it will probably say so on the bag. We use stone-milled whole-wheat flour at my bakery, but you can buy good-quality whole-wheat flour from mainstream producers who use roller mills.

Wheat Gluten

This is an additive sometimes used in large commercial bakeries. Added wheat gluten (sometimes called vital wheat gluten) assists the physical structure of a dough that is intensively mixed and undergoes a short, fast fermentation. This ingredient is not in bread to make the loaf taste better. It's there to make breads rise higher when other additive ingredients are in the dough (multigrain mixes, for example) and can "improve" less-expensive low-protein flour mixes for the commercial baker. Added wheat gluten may improve the rise and allow for speedier production in large commercial bakeries, but there are many questions about what this extra gluten does to the people who eat it. In my opinion, wheat gluten as an added ingredient has no place in the home kitchen (or any bread that I eat) because it does nothing for flavor and it adds to your digestive load. Check the ingredients label on the bread you buy.

Rye Flour

Several recipes in this book use rye flour, one of my favorite flours to blend into a bread for its flavor. The only problem: rye has very weak gluten. A bread made up of 100 percent rye flour will create fermentation gases but the gluten is so weak it doesn't hold on to much of that gas, so the bread is very dense. A few years ago, when Nathan Myhrvold and Francisco Migoya were working on *Modernist Bread*, I learned from them that the quality of rye grown in the United States doesn't match that of rye grown for bakers in European countries; it's a different strain. European rye flour holds the rise better than ours. American rye flour was originally planted most often as a cover crop and used for animal feed. Priorities were different, and, as always, bakers worked with what they could buy. We still do!

To compensate for American rye's weak gluten, I max out at 50 percent rye in the total flour bill (see pages 99 and 221 for two 50 percent rye recipes). And I prefer to fill out the flour blend with white bread flour that is in a higher protein range than all-purpose flour.

Rye can also sometimes create problems in a levain culture that will destroy the gluten in the bread dough. The entire mass just collapses. It is an infrequent occurrence, and I don't want to single out any brand that has been associated with this issue. I've experienced this at my bakery and therefore stick with wheat flour in the sourdough culture and use rye flour only in the final dough. Just be aware that if you think it'd be a cool idea to put rye flour in the levain, it might work, but it might not. When it's a fail, it acts like gluten-eating enzymes have gone wild and destroyed the entire structure. The levain becomes soupy, or it just breaks apart and it's clearly not right.

At the store, you may find rye flour labeled either "light rye," "dark rye," and, less frequently, "whole rye." Dark and whole rye flours can be used interchangeably in my recipes. These flours made from the whole rye berry will have more rye flavor than light rye. Light rye is the rye equivalent of white wheat flour; it is the endosperm of the rye berry without the germ or the bran. This is the flour that I recommend for the New York–Style Rye Bread with Caraway, but dark rye will work fine in that recipe, too, with a stronger flavor and a little denser loaf. Dark rye flour is the rye equivalent of whole-wheat flour; the flour in the bag is from the whole rye berry: the endosperm, the germ, and the rye

bran all together. Dark rye flour blends the bran and the germ of the rye back in with the endosperm but in ratios known only to the miller. If you find a bag of rye flour labeled "whole rye," it should be whole grain with proportions of all the rye elements equal to the original rye berry. If you can find stone-milled rye flour, you should buy it, bake with it, and see how it compares with standard roller-milled and reconstituted dark rye flour.

Ancient Wheat Grains, Heirloom Wheat Varieties, and Delicious Modern Wheat Varieties

If you want better bread, it's time to go beyond the white bread flour, all-purpose flour, whole-wheat flour, and rye flour choices you typically find at the supermarket. The ancient wheats, heirloom wheats, and some new delicious modern varieties are all newly available to consumers in the last decade, and I want to share information about them to let you know how you can use them in this book's recipes. We don't have a single word that sufficiently groups these wheat varieties as one because they all have different lineages. "Craft wheat" doesn't really fit the bill. But what these wheats do have in common is that they taste very good, are often produced by the same quality-conscious millers, and are often interchangeable in my recipes. Try Rouge de Bordeaux or Sonoran White wheat in my recipes written for emmer and einkorn flour, or try substituting in recipes that call for whole-wheat or spelt flour. Some may be a little more or less absorbent than others, some will have stronger or weaker gluten, but you will get good results and delicious bread that is distinctive from bread made with mass-market flour. Imagine if you had ever eaten only one kind of tomato your whole life and

suddenly you tried a ripe heirloom tomato. It's like that.

Let's hope that demand for flour such as this will drive more production of these heritage-grain and modern delicious flours. Almost every mill that I've run across uses stone milling (see page 10) to make flour from spelt, emmer, einkorn, Red Fife, and other high-quality grains. You can enjoy the varietal characteristics of different kinds of wheat by buying flour direct from many craft mills around the country (they are a little more expensive) or by milling your own. The bread from them can be fantastic.

MILLING YOUR OWN

The act of milling wheat kernels (also called wheat berries) into flour is easy enough—if you have a motorized mill, that is. Hand cranking? Well, you're welcome to try it! The mill is a bit of an investment. I have a KoMo mill. Mockmill is another brand. It's good to think beyond just bread if you are going to buy one of these. How about pasta from fresh-milled flour? Or maybe sweets: cookies, brownies, cakes, and tart shells. Puff pastry. Gougères, yum. It comes down to how much time you enjoy spending in your kitchen and if you have some extra money to spend on a mill that makes the effort worth that time. There are some wonderful books about the subject of baking with fresh-milled whole grains too: *Peter Reinhart's Whole Grain Breads* and *Flour Lab* by Adam Leonti are two excellent choices. Kim Boyce's *Good to the Grain* won a James Beard Award and is a good reference as well.

Ancient Wheat Grains

Einkorn, emmer, and spelt—these original wheat forebears predate Plato and Aristotle, going back thousands of years to their origins in the Fertile Crescent. They are genetically simpler and distinct

from the modern-day wheat varieties they evolved into. These ancient grains do have gluten-producing proteins, yet the gluten from them is weaker than in modern wheat varieties, especially for einkorn and emmer. But the flavor! Nutty and rich. The emmer, einkorn, and spelt recipes in this book make bread with a more intense grain flavor than standard white and whole-wheat flour will produce. These grains could make beer and whiskey too.

Heirloom Wheat Varieties

At what point do old varieties of wheat become new again? This seems like a silly question, but what has happened is older varieties of really good-tasting wheat were largely displaced more than one hundred years ago by modern varieties that scale better for high-volume farming, milling, and baking.

Red Fife, Turkey Red, Rouge de Bordeaux, and others are a collection of wheat varieties that were commonly grown prior to the late 1800s, when breeders produced higher-yielding crops and rail transport enabled industrial-scale milling, and that changed everything. High yield and disease resistance are key factors in wheat farming for good reason. The goal is to feed the people. The farmers plant what is marketable. Wheat-seed stocks are bred for yield, disease resistance, and performance in the mill and in large-scale bakeries. They are planted based on what the biggest customers want to buy.

When bread baking moved from the home kitchen to industrial bakeries in the early 1900s, the desire for high-rising, sliced, and packaged white bread led to further varietal breeding of the wheat crops, and more large mills in order to meet the demand. It's completely understandable how we got here. The United States once had more than twenty thousand commercial grain mills for a population that was just 15 percent of today's citizenship. We now have a few hundred mills, not thousands. In Sosland Publishing's 2019 *Grain & Milling Annual*, Pennsylvania led all other states with fourteen commercial flour mills. Kansas and California had twelve each.

Yet here we are in the future, with many smaller farms growing some of these heirloom wheat varieties and ancient wheat grains, like emmer, einkorn, and spelt. Some have found or helped create niche markets to produce wheat that just tastes better and meets the needs of artisan bakers, chefs, and local markets. Many are family-owned small farms that work in cooperative arrangements to use the same seed stock (and sometimes the same farming methods, such as no-till wheat farming) and pool their harvests to sell their wheat to a small number of mills that are new but using old-school stone-milling methods. Although this is still a very small percentage of the wheat that is grown in the United States (and other countries too), people like us are lucky these farmers and millers are out there—and that their numbers are growing. We have a greater choice of quality grains and flours than even a decade ago. And thanks to an online marketplace, you are not limited to what's available at your local grocery store.

Modern Delicious Wheat Varieties

There are thousands of wheat varieties. Some are bred for flavor and good baking qualities, and those are the ones that I'm interested in. It's great to see this breakaway from the mainstream to create another set of marketable wheat varieties that have benefits for the farmer and on the table. You can especially thank Dr. Stephen Jones, the founder and director of the Breadlab at Washington State University in the Skagit Valley. He and his team have been influential in the development of many of these grains, and much of their work has been crossbreeding to make new varieties that, when successful, end up in farmers' fields. These varieties are crossbred for better yields, disease resistance, and flavor too. Good craft mills are turning them into stone-ground flour that you and I can bake from. Edison flour is a fun example bred by Merrill Lewis, a retired English professor in Bellingham, Washington, for the Pacific Northwest climate! If the wheat works for the farmer ("yield, cost, and ability to sell," as the Breadlab's website succinctly puts it), the miller, the baker, and the consumers, everybody wins.

Good Grains Need a Good Mill

I think my enthusiasm for craft mills, heirloom grains, and ancient grains is clear. There are people behind these bags of flour who are owners and employees—no stockholders, just *stakeholders*. As a baker, I'm always looking for flour that can make a new great-tasting bread in my repertoire, or that can improve a bread I already make. And I really like a connection to the people who produce it. Almost all these farm mills are new within the last decade. They are meeting a market that does for wheat what farmers' markets have done for farm-fresh produce—bring better ingredients, fresh from the farm, to the home plate. Here are a few quotes straight from the farms that bring the message home from their points of view.

■ Camas Country Mill, Eugene, Oregon

When Camas Country first opened its doors in 2011, we were the first mill of our kind to operate in the Willamette Valley in nearly eighty years. Grist mills once peppered the landscape, particularly along waterways, with mills in even the smallest communities. Over time, as the success of the seed industry pushed locally consumed grains to the margins, local mills also faded away from the valley, and factory flour came to dominate pantry and grocery shelves across the Pacific Northwest.

The first rumblings of a local mill enterprise started in Tom Hunton's mind as commodity crop prices were buffeted by the stormy economy during the recession. Having raised grass seed, vegetable and cover crop seed, and wheat for export for decades, Tom decided it was time to diversify the family farm even further and try something virtually unheard of for a midsize farm—grow grain for the local regional market. (Tom is pictured opposite, holding an image of his grandfather's bakery wagon in Denmark in the 1920s.) Meetings with the Southern Willamette Valley Bean and Grain Project and consulting with university plant breeders led to wheat test-plots on Hunton's farm. Defying conventional wisdom, that first harvest proved that valley-grown hard red and white spring wheat had sufficient protein to meet the needs of commercial bakers. Not content to grow the grain and navigate financially and environmentally damaging shipping to a processor elsewhere, the Huntons decided to build their own mill.

Since then, more local and regional farmers have joined us in growing grains and legumes that are processed or packed at Camas Country, and more than 2 million pounds of flour runs through our mill annually. We now supply ten Oregon school districts with whole-grain flour, as well as packaging a complete-protein lentil-barley soup mix for our local food bank and supplying home and commercial kitchens throughout the West.

Farmer Ground Flour, Hudson Valley, New York

Our system consists of several stone mills running in sequence, which is designed to gradually and gently grind the kernels into flour. Meadows Mills in North Carolina cut the twenty-inch and thirty-inch granite stones. The vertical stones run at relatively slow RPMs, dividing the workload between different machines to minimize heat and physical pressure.

We farm and mill in New York state—not the arid West or vast fields of the former tall-grass prairie. Because of our climate and relatively small farms, producing organic grain of milling quality is a challenge. Similar to farmers' markets, mills can be levers in building a regional food system. We are motivated to help New York state farmers step out of the volatile commodity market by building long-term relationships and providing a stable price and consistent market.

Janie's Mill, Ashkum, Illinois

Stone milling is an art and a science. Key to our high-quality products are the skill of our miller and the modern science behind the ancient, time-tested technology of stone milling.

Our two stone mills were custom-made by Engsko, a Danish company that has been in the mill business for over a century. Our modern mill looks different from the centuries-old Italian mill, but both work by feeding whole grain kernels between stationary and rotating millstones. We carefully monitor the temperature of the stones to ensure they stay cool and preserve all the nutrition of the whole kernel—including the bran and germ, with all their essential proteins, oils, vitamins, and minerals. Even our sifted flours contain 70 to 90 percent of the whole kernel, so you get more flavor and more nutrition.

Equipment

Any job is easier when you have the right tools. Some are essential and some just make the project go smoother with less hassle. I like the feeling of everything being in its place, and the task at hand is faster and much more efficient when you're not looking for this and that throughout the process. If you have used *Flour Water Salt Yeast*, you'll have almost everything you need already except for the bread pans: one or two sizes of open pans and another with a lid. The items that I recommend are discussed roughly in order of use.

Dough Tubs

For most of the recipes in this book, I ask you to mix the dough by hand and let it rise in the same container. It is easy and efficient.

6-QUART / 6-LITER SIZE

I like to use a 6-quart see-through vessel with volume markings on the side (e.g., 2-quart, 4-quart, 6-quart) and a matching lid. If you have one of these, the process is unfussy and leaves little to clean up. Rounded containers work much better than squared-edge options because of the ease of

EVOLUTIONS IN BREAD

mixing in them by hand. Dry flour and dough bits get caught in squared-off corners; but if that's all you have, it's not a deal breaker. Almost all the doughs in this book are mixed by hand (the exceptions are the three enriched doughs: Brioche, Butter Bread, and Shokupan, or Japanese Milk Bread). Having the right container—I call it a dough tub, and you can search on that term online—makes everything else about the process easier.

This size is big enough for the book's single-loaf batch yields. Every dough needs a couple of quick, easy folds (see page 41) in the hour after you mix it to develop strength so the loaf will rise higher and won't flop too much over the sides of its baking pan. The 6-quart tub will let you put the folds in the dough quickly and easily without removing it from the tub.

The volume markings on the tub will help you decide when it's time to remove the dough to make up a loaf, as I guide you on the amount of volume expansion in its first rise. I write to let it expand to "two and a half times" or "two and a half to three times" its original volume, and that involves some guesswork. It is more accurate and reliable for me to tell you to remove the dough and make up your loaf when the dough has risen to the level of a marking that you can reference on the side of the tub. Often the point of rise in the recipes is just shy (about ¼ inch in some, ½ inch in others) of the 2-quart line. Go ahead and mark your own measurement lines on your dough tub. Easy enough!

The recipe timelines are just a guide and work reliably in my house in Oregon at 70°F / 21°C. But if I lived in Houston, Texas, or Charleston, South Carolina, both hot and humid climates, the dough would rise faster unless the A/C were turned up. Or someone who lives in Scotland in a cold farmhouse might find it takes twice the time for the dough to rise to its needed amount. The difference in pace of the rise in cold temperatures versus warm is huge. In all the recipes, I give time estimates for bulk dough fermentation, and you can use that as a guide, especially if your kitchen is also about 70°F / 21°C. But I really want your decision to be based on the amount of rise in the dough, and that is easiest to represent if we are both using the same dough tub. If you plan to bake frequently, it's well worth the small expense. The markings on the outside will give you confidence as you follow the recipe.

If you use my first book and bought a 12-quart dough tub to make two-loaf batches of bread dough, you'll already know what I mean. And if you still have that tub, you can use it here for a single batch as well, although it is best suited for two-loaf batches.

2-QUART / 2-LITER SIZE

If you want to make your own sourdough culture and follow the natural-levain recipes in this book, a 2-quart rounded container with volume markings on the side and a lid is the perfect size and shape. When you start a new levain culture in this vessel, it seems a little big at first; but by the time you finish, it is just right. The start-up culture that I have takes about a week to create from scratch and then it will be stored in the refrigerator to be plucked from as needed to make bread. The 2-quart container that I use fits easily in the refrigerator. I have a couple of these, as this is also the perfect size for starters, biga, and popcorn. There are plenty of food storage containers out there.

Dough Tub Alternatives

Large mixing bowls can work in place of a dough tub, so long as they are big enough— at least 12 inches wide at the brim and 5 or 6 inches high, with an 8-quart capacity. You can cover them with plastic wrap or invert another slightly smaller or same-size bowl on top to form a lid.

Scale

These recipes will give you predictable results when you use a digital scale to measure flour, water, salt, and yeast. It's easy to do; don't be afraid of precision. Scales are not very expensive and will allow you to mix dough with the confidence that everything was measured accurately. I like scales with a pull-out display for easy reading. But there are many options and, at the end of the day, I'd recommend

you shop mostly on price. If you need to buy a new digital kitchen scale, check out its measuring range and weight limit, and verify it will measure in both grams and ounces. A 5-pound weight limit is good enough for this book's recipes. Measuring in 1-gram increments is the minimum degree of accuracy that I recommend. There are many affordable scales that fit these guidelines.

Measuring ingredients by weight works better than measuring with cups and tablespoons. Your 360 grams of water will be the same as mine, but I'm less confident that you and I would come up with exactly the same amount of water if I told you to measure out 1½ cups. An extra splash of water can make a big difference in the consistency of a dough. The same goes for a tablespoon more or less of flour, which can affect the texture of finished dough. If you use a digital kitchen scale, your baked goods will reliably turn out better and will be more worth the time and effort you put into them.

Measuring salt in these recipes is another good reason to use a scale. Different brands of salt may have varying grain sizes, and 2 teaspoons of one salt may not weigh the same as 2 teaspoons of another salt, especially if one is coarse grained. It'll be a big difference and greatly affect the bread you make.

Yeast is another story; ¼ teaspoon instant dried yeast conveniently weighs very close to 1 gram. This is one exception that I can count on as an accurate alternative to my use-a-scale rule. Scales that measure in single gram increments aren't always accurate on the small 2- to 3-gram weights that I have for yeast in this book, so a ¼ teaspoon is the better way to measure unless you have a scale that measures to tenths to hundredths of a gram. If you want the fine scale, they are not expensive and their product descriptions will say "0.1g or 0.01g."

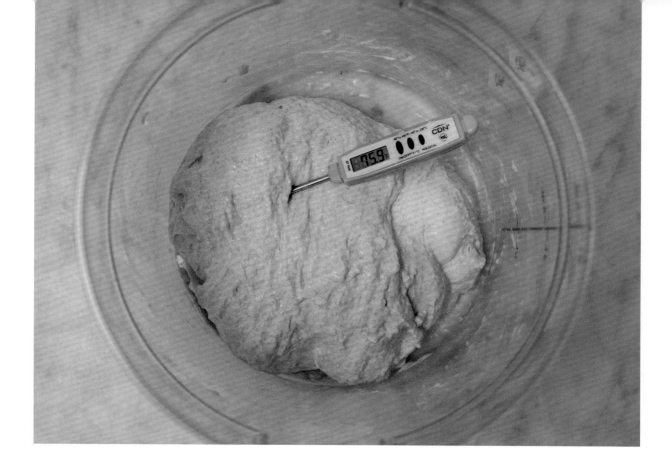

Instant-Read Probe Thermometer

In my first book, I wrote, "Think of time and temperature as ingredients." It remains my essential piece of guidance in bread baking. Using a digital probe thermometer, often labeled as a "meat thermometer" (this works), ensures that you work with the water temperature that I recommend in the recipes. If you use the recipe's listed-temperature water and room-temperature flour for your dough mix, your dough will rise on a predictable timeline. Everything in the recipe will fall into place. You can stick the thermometer into your dough to see if the dough is at the temperature the recipe recommends, usually around 75°F / 24°C. Colder dough is going to rise much more slowly. Warmer dough will rise too fast. The thermometer, which should cost less than $15, will have other uses in the kitchen as well, especially for measuring the temperature of cooked meat. Taylor, Cooper-Atkins, and CDN are brands that I can recommend.

Bread Pans and Dutch Ovens

Most of the breads in this book are designed to be pan breads, but a key feature is that they can also be Dutch-oven loaves. One dough fits any of these three kinds of baking vessels: open pan, lidded pan, and Dutch oven.

OPEN PAN

I used two pan sizes in my recipe testing for open-pan breads. The smaller pan, made by USA Pan, is nonstick and measures 8½ by 4½ by 2¾ inches. The product description says "1-pound loaf pan," but my one-loaf recipes make a little more than 2 pounds of dough. The loaf rises high above the rim of this pan, and I like the effect of that. The bottom half of the loaf bakes a little bit more compressed than in the larger pan that I tested, which measured 9¼ by 5 by 3⅛ inches. I ended up using the larger pan more because I get a little bit more open crumb and a slightly larger loaf. (A finished loaf pops right out if the pan gets a spray ahead of time.) The pan, even if it's a nonstick, does sometimes need cooking spray, as the dough can flop over the edges a little and grab the rim. Both these sizes and anything in between will work fine to make your breads that rise and bake in an open pan.

LIDDED PAN

When you bake in a pan with the lid on, if the pan is properly sized for the amount of dough in your loaf, the dough will rise all the way up to the lid as it bakes. The loaf will then have the exact shape of the pan on the top, bottom, and sides with squared edges. The crust that forms is very thin. This loaf is a good choice for sandwiches, canapés, French toast, and more. I can recommend the CHEFMADE non-stick carbon-steel loaf pan with lid, which measures 8.4 by 4.8 by 4.5 inches.

DUTCH-OVEN POT WITH LID

Baking bread in a preheated Dutch oven gives you a crusty, artisan-style loaf that looks like it came from a great bakery. This is the style of bread that I featured in *Flour Water Salt Yeast*. Size is important. My loaves are sized to bake best in a 4-quart Dutch oven. Many more affordable Dutch ovens are on the market than in the past. I've long been a fan of Lodge Cast Iron. Enameled cast-iron Dutch ovens are colorful and easy to maintain. Make sure yours has a knob on the lid that can handle an oven temperature of 500°F / 260°C. My Dutch ovens are 10 inches in diameter at the top and 4 inches deep. If you have a 5-quart Dutch oven, it will also work. The dough will spread out more than in a 4-quart Dutch oven, so the loaves will be a bit wider and not quite as tall and rounded as those in the photos of this book. Also, breads may not split open on top in the same way they do in a 4-quart model, since there will be less vertical pressure as the loaves get their oven spring.

Proofing Basket

For Dutch-oven loaves, you need a proofing basket that holds the dough during its second rise, after the dough is shaped into a loaf. When the dough is ready to bake, you tamp it onto a countertop, then transfer it to a preheated Dutch oven. There are many more options on the market than there were ten years ago, and the prices are better too. The right size for these recipes is 9 inches in diameter at the top and 3½ inches deep. A proofing basket will last a lifetime. Linen-lined baskets are a classic choice, although I prefer to remove the linen because I like the aesthetic of the marks from the basket's wicker pattern on the loaves. You can also improvise a proofing basket using a bowl of approximately the same dimensions lined with a flour-dusted, lint-free tea towel.

Odds and Ends

Following are a few more items that aid the process of bread baking.

- You'll want a pair of oven mitts or folded thick kitchen towels for handling hot bread pans and Dutch ovens. Make sure the mitts you buy are safe for handling something at a temperature of 500°F / 260°C. Give them or a folded towel a test with a quick set down to make sure.
- An oven thermometer comes in handy, since home ovens rarely deliver the exact temperature you dial in. Mine runs about 25°F / 15°C cooler, so when I set it to 500°F / 260°C, I actually get 475°F / 245°C.
- You'll need something to cover the proofing baskets after you have shaped the loaves. I like to use nonperforated plastic bags, which allow the loaves to proof overnight in the refrigerator without drying out. I reuse clean bags that I get at the produce section of the market for this purpose.

CHAPTER 2
METHODS & TECHNIQUES

This is the how-to part of the book that describes the instructions in each of the recipes. Readers of my first book will be familiar with many of the steps here: Mix dough by hand in the container it will rise in. Let the dough rest in an initial mix (autolyse) before adding salt and yeast and then complete the final dough mix. Use a scale to measure ingredients, and a thermometer to measure water temperature and dough temperature. It's that simple.

The Setup

This chapter is going to give you long-form instructions and deep knowledge for each step so you have what you need to know. These methods and techniques are described and sometimes abbreviated in each recipe. Here, I'll also go over how to make artisan pan loaves or Dutch-oven loaves from the same recipe. The first step in any recipe is to assemble the items and ingredients that you'll use to make the bread.

- Digital kitchen scale
- ¼ teaspoon (to measure small amounts of yeast)
- Water container, 2-quart or larger
- Digital probe thermometer
- Small measuring container for salt measurements
- 6-quart dough tub or equivalent-size bowl
- Proofing basket, if baking a Dutch-oven loaf
- Flour (one or more types, depending on the recipe)
- Fine sea salt
- Instant dried yeast
- Levain or starter

With everything in its place, you only have to focus on the requirements of the recipe and not interrupt the process by looking for things you need in the moment. It's all right there.

Most of the recipes suggest the use of a levain as an optional ingredient. The recipes work well without it, but they will taste better with it. Yet there will be times when you don't have this secret sauce available or haven't made one yet. You can bake bread without it, don't worry. Still, I recommend that you make a levain from scratch. It's an easy process, just 5 minutes a day for 1 week. Once done, you can store it in the refrigerator to be used in the recipes (it needs a refresh feeding once every 7 or 10 days).

> **Terms**
>
> I use the words *levain, culture, and sourdough* interchangeably, as you will likely hear other people use each of these terms. It's all the same thing; a culture of natural yeasts that leaven the dough.

About These Wet, Slack Doughs

My bread doughs use more water than what you find in a bread-machine recipe or in traditional American baking. Yet these wet doughs are typical of the best artisan bakeries (and of my first book) because of the flavor and texture that comes from them. Bread made from wetter doughs will last longer, taste better, and have a lighter texture. The doughs will be gassy and lively as they rise. They feel different from traditional bread doughs, more wet and goopy at the beginning. You might think there is an error in either the recipe or in the measurements. But if you look at the photos of the dough mix (see pages 37, 39, and 40) and how the dough is folded, you'll see that's what it's supposed to look like.

The reasons for this kind of wet dough are:

- The bread lasts longer without the addition of preservatives. These loaves will keep a good 5 days if stored in an airtight container or plastic bag.

- Bread made from a stiffer dough (less water in the dough) will be denser than the more lightly textured breads in this book.
- More water in the dough encourages an active fermentation. Your bread can rise slowly but surely, starting with a smaller amount of yeast and no sugar, compared with many standard pan-bread recipes. All of this improves the flavor and lightens the texture of the loaf.
- The bread has a better texture when toasted—crisp on the outside, soft and tender on the inside.

This type of dough needs some help during the early part of its rise. The folding technique that I recommend is used widely in good craft bakeries to ensure wet dough has the structure it needs to bake into a nice loaf without collapsing. It works like this. You pull and stretch one side of the dough until it resists and then reverse direction and drape it, folding the pulled dough over the rest, like folding a packet. Do this with each portion of dough and it will form a rounded mass—a bread-dough balloon. This folding has intertwined the gluten strands in the dough, adding more complexity to their overall structure. The result is a dough that can resist flattening out. Do this a few times during the first rise and the dough will have enough strength to hold its form.

How to Read the Recipe Tables

The recipes in this book list flour first, followed by water, salt, and yeast, reflecting the relative quantities of these ingredients in the recipe. Then, added ingredients are listed at the bottom of each recipe: nuts (50% Rye Bread with Walnuts), nut meal (Hazelnut Bread), black rice flour (Black Bread), corn kernels (Corn [Flour] Bread), tea-soaked raisins and pecans (Raisin-Pecan Bread), butter (Butter Bread!), and more. Here's a quick explanation of the information in the different columns of the recipe tables, followed by an example.

Ingredients and amounts are listed by weight, the preferred way to measure for accuracy, which is easy to do with a kitchen scale. For convenience, if you have not yet purchased a scale, the amounts in volume measurements appear alongside the weights. The third column, labeled "baker's percentage," is very useful to understand the recipe at a quick glance, and the more you bake and become familiar with the numbers, the more you'll appreciate the percentages as a point of reference.

You don't need to understand baker's percentage notations to use these recipes. The bread will be just as good either way. But they do help to understand the recipe better, and that has value when you compare a recipe here with others you already know. They also allow you to understand how 4 or 5 percent more or less water in a recipe will make a big difference in the texture of the dough. If you want to vary the flour blend of a recipe that you are using, you'll have a similar point of reference once you have a feel for this notation.

The baker's percentages used in baking books often vary from author to author or, in my case, from book to book. In classic form, the baker's percentage divides every ingredient weight by the weight of the total flour in the recipe. All the flour in the dough mix, added up, always equals 100 percent. If you have 1,000 grams of flour and 750 grams of water in the dough, it's 75 percent water. Likewise, 20 grams of salt against 1,000 grams of flour equals 2 percent, a standard amount of salt in bread doughs—though I prefer a slight uptick, to 2.2 percent salt, for taste.

I introduced a slight hiccup in this book by having most recipes use an optional 100 grams of refrigerated levain. The recipes work with or without it (but they taste better with it!). Using this 100 grams of sourdough to flavor the loaf will slightly change the baker's percentages in the recipes compared with not using it. To ease the understanding, I am using the percentages that do not include the levain.

As a quick example, in my 50% Emmer or Einkorn Bread, I list the emmer or einkorn flour as 50 percent of the total flour, which is 250 grams of the total 500 grams. When you also use the 100 grams of levain, half of which is white bread flour, the 250 grams of emmer or einkorn flour in this recipe will actually be 45.5 percent of the total flour in the recipe (550 grams). I chose not to give you columns to represent either/or values to avoid what seems to me an unnecessary complication.

Likewise, when the optional levain is used, the salt will equal 2 percent and the hydration of the dough will increase slightly.

You may also notice that the water amount and its corresponding percentage (referred to as the hydration of the dough) changes depending on the flour blend. The 50% Emmer or Einkorn Bread has 85 percent water because these whole-grain flours, especially when freshly milled, soak up a lot more water than a bag of white bread flour. My White Bread recipe has 74 percent water in the dough. Both doughs will have a similar consistency, even with this big difference in water. That's my goal—to have most of these pan breads end up with a very similar consistency. The amount of water needs to vary to achieve that, depending on the absorbency of the flour in each recipe.

How to Do It in Eight Steps

The process for making bread as described here will become automatic after a few times of doing it. Just follow the instructions as written. It is easy to be good at this! Go ahead, dive right in.

Step 1: Autolyse

The word *autolyse* is derived from the French *autolysis*. It is an approach commonly used in good craft bakeries and is a way to let the flour absorb the water in wet doughs before adding salt and leavening. Blend just the flour and the water in the recipe, then let it rest for 20 minutes or so before mixing in the salt and yeast. If you are using the refrigerated levain, I found it works well to include it in the autolyse mixture—it takes a long time for its yeast to wake up and it integrates easier at this stage.

The autolyse process is beneficial for home bakers because it allows for improved gluten development in hand-mixed doughs, resulting in better gas retention and better volume in the finished loaf (gluten is formed from proteins, mostly glutenin and gliadin, that are in the flour). When flour and water are mixed, the protein strands elongate and intertwine at the same time that the flour's starch is absorbing water. When hand mixing, you can feel the difference between a dough that went through this process and one that didn't. Autolysed dough already has some of the structure that a dough mixed all at once, without the autolyse, doesn't have until later in its development. Following are the actions to make up the autolyse dough-mix stage in the recipes.

A. Fill a container with water at the right temperature. Most of the one-loaf recipes in this book use between 370 grams and 425 grams water at a specified temperature. Fill a 2-quart or so container about halfway with water at a guessed-at temperature from the tap that feels close to the target (usually around 90°F / 32°C), then measure the temp with your digital probe thermometer and adjust up or down, adding colder or hotter water until the container has water at or near to the recommended temperature.

B. Weigh the water for the recipe. Turn on your scale. Put your 6-quart dough tub or equivalent container on it and then press "tare" or "zero" to zero it out. Pour the target-temperature water into the dough tub to reach the weight of water specified in the recipe.

C. If you have a levain, scale it into the dough tub containing the measured water by keeping the tub on the scale, hitting "tare" or "zero," and pouring the levain (usually 100 grams) directly and carefully into the water until you reach the weight the recipe calls for. Pinch the levain with wet fingers to stop the flow.

D. Stir in the levain with your fingers, swooshing it around and blending it nearly completely with the water.

E. If you are confident, keep the tub on the scale, hit "tare" or "zero," and add all the flour. If you're nervous or new to the process, to be safe, remove the dough tub from the scale, set another dry container on the scale, hit "tare" or "zero," measure the flour specified in the recipe, and then add all the flour to your 6-quart tub.

F. With the tub off the scale, hold it with one hand and use your other hand to mix the flour and water into a dough. You will know the autolyse mix is done when there are no longer any loose bits of dry flour visible in the dough tub. Your working hand will get a little sticky with dough. Don't worry—you need to get used to using your hand as an implement. Even though dough bits are sticking to you (just like they would stick to a dough hook), keep mixing until the flour and water are integrated. Any dough clumps should be pinched through with your hand. After mixing, use your free hand to squeegee the dough that's stuck to your working hand into the tub.

G. Measure the recipe amount of fine sea salt on your kitchen scale (place an empty container on the scale, hit "tare" or "zero," add salt until you hit the specified weight) and sprinkle the salt fairly evenly over the wet dough. (It will partially dissolve.) Then repeat this step with the dry yeast. If you are unsure of your scale's accuracy with small measurements, you can use a leveled ¼ teaspoon to equal 1 gram yeast. This is a very reliable approximation that will give you fine results. Sprinkle the measured yeast on top of the dough. Do not worry about the yeast coming into contact with the salt; it won't be a problem. It is a persistent myth in home baking that salt and yeast should not touch, but these two ingredients share space in the bread dough anyway, right? The concentrations of salt to yeast need to be much higher for this to be an issue, and the coating on dried yeast protects it until it dissolves in the dough along with the salt. Put the lid on the container and let the dough rest for 15 to 20 minutes.

Add 100 grams levain to the water and swoosh it around.

Then measure in the flour.

Mix it all together by hand.

Mix until it forms a dough.

Weigh the salt and yeast.

Sprinkle the salt and yeast on top and let rest 15 minutes.

Step 2: Final Dough Mix (Use Your Hand!)

Hand mixing the final dough should take 5 minutes or less. I prefer to mix it by hand in the dough tub, rather than kneading it on the counter or using an electric mixer. It's simpler, faster, entails less cleanup, and is fully effective. The dough stays in the same tub from the autolyse step until it is shaped into a loaf 3 or so hours later, depending on the recipe format. Why make it more complicated when it doesn't need to be? Here are the actions that make up the final dough mix stage in the recipes.

A. Set yourself up with the water container you used to measure water for the recipe, filled partway with warm water for this step. Dip your working hand (right hand if you are right-handed) fully into the water to wet it before mixing the dough. A wet hand helps keep the dough from sticking to you and makes this process much easier.

B. Grab the dough tub with your dry hand. Then reach underneath the dough with your wet hand and grab about one-fourth of it. Gently stretch this section and fold it over the top to the other side of the dough. Repeat three more times with the remaining dough until the salt and yeast are fully enclosed. See the photos for an example, and pay attention to how my hand is grabbing and stretching the dough—most of my hand is underneath, my thumb is on top. Apply pressure with the flat parts of your hand and fingers, not your fingertips.

C. Now, using a pincerlike grip with your thumb and forefinger, squeeze big chunks of dough and then tighten your grip to cut through it. Do this repeatedly, working through the entire mass of dough, essentially breaking it into five or six pieces. With your other hand, adjust the tub while you're mixing to give your working hand a good angle of attack. (I learned this "pincer method" in 1999 at the San Francisco Baking Institute, and it is still the best way I know to mix one- or two-loaf batches of dough by hand.)

D. After you have pincer cut through the dough five or six times, stretch and fold it over itself a few times. Then once again cut through it five or six times and fold it over itself a few more times. Repeat this process, alternating between cutting and folding, until you feel and see that all the ingredients are fully integrated. Dip your mixing hand back into the container of warm water three or four times throughout this process to rewet it and prevent the dough from sticking to you. If you don't, the dough will be sticky and hard to work. It is normal to feel the granularity of the salt and yeast as you mix; using a wet hand for mixing will help the salt and yeast dissolve. For me, it takes 2 or 3 minutes. For first timers, it will probably take about 5 minutes to be sure everything is well mixed and you've done enough folds during the mix process to build up the gluten. Let the dough rest for a few minutes, then fold for another 30 seconds or until the dough tightens up. That's it for mixing!

E. At the end of the mix, measure the temperature of the dough with your probe thermometer. In most of the recipes in this book, the target temperature is 75°F / 24°C. Write down the final mix temperature and the time. If the dough temperature is well below 75°F / 24°C, it will take longer to rise. Dough that is warmer will rise faster. In all cases, you'll need to follow the recipe guidance for how much rise to expect in the dough before moving on to the next step. Cover the tub, let the dough rise in an area that is close to 70°F / 21°C, and you can reliably follow the timelines in the recipe.

Wet your hand so the dough doesn't stick.

Grab the dough from underneath and fold over, about one quarter segment at a time.

Continue folding the dough over itself to fully enclose the salt and yeast.

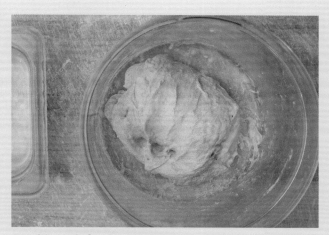

Now it's ready for the next step.

The pincer technique: Cut through the dough between your thumb and forefinger.

Pincer cut five or six times across the dough, then fold it and repeat the cut and fold several times.

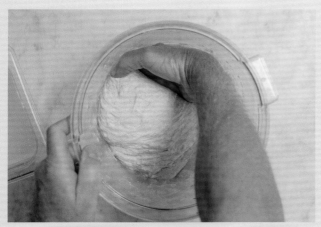

Fold the dough during its first rise. Use a wet hand.

Grab about one-fourth of the dough from underneath.

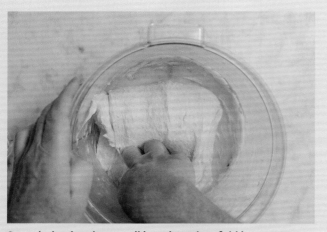

Stretch the dough up until it resists, then fold it over.

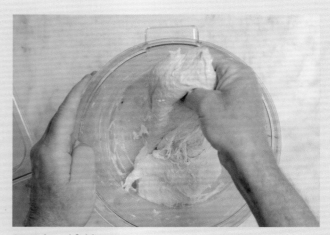

Stretch and fold.

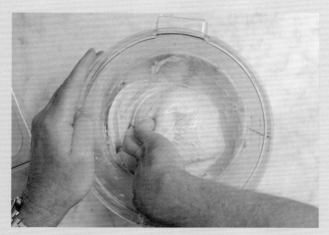

Stretch and fold.

Done! Let it rest. Most of the recipes ask for two or three folds.

Step 3: Fold & First Rise

Because my doughs are wet and loose, they need a little help, so folding is an essential step during their first rise. Folding the dough helps develop the gluten that gives the dough its strength and contributes to good volume in the final loaf. Each fold takes about 1 minute at first, and just seconds after you have done it a few times. The recipes in this book need just one, two, or three folds. You'll be able to recognize when to apply the next fold based on how relaxed the dough has become—in time it goes from being a ball with structure to lying flattened out in the tub. With each fold, the dough firms up a bit; I try to work in all the folds during the first hour of the rise.

A. The action here is just like the folds during mixing in Step 2. Dip your working hand fully into the container of warm water to wet it so the dough doesn't stick to you. With your wet hand, reach underneath the dough and pull about one-fourth of it out and up to stretch it as far as you can until you feel resistance, then fold it over the top to the other side of the dough. Repeat four or five times, working around the dough until it has tightened into a ball.

B. When the dough relaxes a bit and flattens in the bottom of the tub, repeat the process for the second fold. After each fold, the dough develops more structure, or strength, than it had before and will therefore take longer to relax completely. The recipe instructions tell you how many folds to apply.

C. Each recipe tells you the amount of rise needed and what it looks like against the volume marking on the 6-quart tub. Usually it's ¼ to ½ inch below the 2-quart line. If you have the 12-quart dough tub that I recommended in *Flour Water Salt Yeast*, you can use it, and the volume markings are equivalent.

Carefully remove the dough from its tub.

Lift the dough out from the bottom, careful not to tear it.

Remove the dough onto a floured surface.

Set it up to the width of your baking pan. Spritz the pan with cooking spray.

Step 4: Remove the Dough from Its Tub

The right way to perform this step is to lift the dough out from underneath and remove it from its tub in one piece.

A. Moderately flour a work surface—you'll need an area about 12 inches wide. Working next to the floured area, flour your hands and gently loosen the dough all the way around the perimeter of the tub, taking care not to let the gluten strands tear. Reach to the bottom of the tub and gently

loosen the bottom of the dough from the tub. It's helpful to toss some flour along the edges of the tub to work underneath the dough and help ease its release. Then turn the tub on its side and use your hands to help gently ease the dough out onto the work surface.

B. If you double the recipe and made a two-loaf batch, sprinkle flour across the middle of the top of the dough where you'll need to cut it. Then divide it into two equal pieces with a dough knife, plastic dough scraper, or kitchen knife.

Step 5: Shape the Loaf

Decision time! Make up your dough into a pan loaf or a Dutch-oven loaf with the following instructions. Take a look at the photos, too, and pay close attention to how I handle the dough.

OPEN AND LIDDED-PAN LOAVES

You'll get better at this with repetition, but baking bread in a pan is pretty forgiving. Even if all you do is just get the dough into the bread pan, you will still get a good loaf. Give your pan a spritz of cooking spray to ensure the loaf pops right out, problem free, even if your pan is nonstick. A long time ago, I had a pair of glass bread pans and, too often, part of the finished loaf was stuck to the glass. The results after prying the loaf out weren't pretty.

A. Stretch and fold the slack dough into something equal to the width of your bread pan. Do your best to grab the dry underneath part of the dough with most of your hand, not your fingertips, as you pick up each side to stretch and fold over itself. The wet and sticky part of the dough is facing up. I always grab the dough with my thumb of either hand on the top of the dough and my palm and fingers grabbing from underneath. Check out the photos to see this.

B. With floured hands, pick up the dough and ease it back down onto the work surface, working it into a somewhat even, rectangular shape. Then stretch the dough, simultaneously pulling it right and left (just spread your hands both ways at the same time to stretch out the dough) until it resists—two to three times its original width—and fold the ends back over each other, creating a "packet" the width of your baking pan. It feels weird the first time. Gets better.

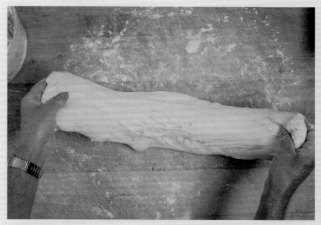

Stretch the dough left and right with floured hands until it resists.

Fold one side inward.

Then fold the other side over to the width of the bread pan.

Roll it up!

Finish rolling it up.

Tighten it up a bit, pull it back toward you to tighten it, but don't stress it.

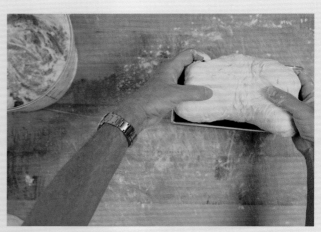

Place it in the pan.

C. Brush off any loose flour from the top of the dough and do a roll-up motion from the bottom up or from top to bottom to form a tube of dough that's about the same width as your baking pan. If the dough goes wider than the pan width, give it another stretch, fold to a little less than the width of the pan, and then give another roll-up motion. *Place the dough seam-up into the pan*. If you are a novice and you can't find the seam (I've seen it happen), just get the dough into the pan. If you are using a lidded pan, you don't need to worry about the seam.

D. Don't stress this part. It takes repeated efforts to learn the hand skills to shape sticky, slack bread dough. The pan does much of the work for you, so if all you can manage is getting the dough into the pan, you're not a failure—it'll work fine. Dough bits will stick to your fingers, and with time you will get used to it. To repeat: *My trick is always to grab the dough by its driest outside and flour-covered bottom parts that aren't so sticky. Just avoid leaving any loose flour inside the dough before you roll it up into the pan's shape.*

DUTCH-OVEN LOAVES

If you know how to round a piece of dough into a ball, you pretty much have this part covered. I like this loaf to be shaped into a medium-tight round with some tension in the dough. Read on for my suggested shaping technique. Be aware that when your dough pieces are sitting on the floured work surface, the underside of the dough will be stretched to become the outside of the loaf; this will help you understand the shaping process. The bottom of each piece of dough is sitting on some flour, so it's not going to be as sticky there. Keeping your hands in contact with that part of the dough is the most important advice I can offer; otherwise, the dough will stick to your hands.

A. Begin by brushing any loose flour off the top of the dough with your hand to avoid getting any loose flour on the inside of the loaf. Using the same technique as in the folding step (Step 3), stretch and fold one-fourth of the dough at a time up and over the top to form a round, gently pulling each segment out until you get to its maximum stretch, then folding it over the top to the opposite side. Repeat, working your way around the dough and forming it into a ball, until the interior is fully enclosed and you have a round with a little tension in it. Flip the round over so the seam is on the work surface in an area cleared of flour—at this point you want the friction, or grip, of a clean surface. You are now looking at the smooth surface of the loaf, which will be faceup in the proofing basket and face-down while the loaf is baking.

B. Cup your hands around the back of the dough ball as you face it. Pull the entire dough ball 6 to 8 inches toward you on the dry, unfloured surface, leading with your pinkie fingers and applying

Shape a fairly tight round of dough.

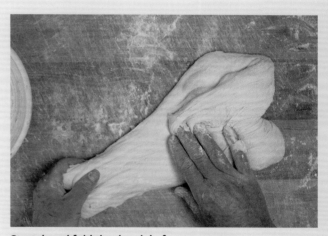
Stretch and fold the dough in four segments.

Stretch until the dough resists, then fold it over like this.

Stretch and fold.

One more to form the round.

Finish forming the round.

Now to tighten it up, on a surface clear of flour, cup your hands around the back of the dough.

Pull back to you, pressing the dough down and toward you. Do it a few times, turning until it's tight.

Place the dough seam (bottom) down into a floured basket or big bowl. Cover.

enough downward pressure so the dough ball grips your work surface and doesn't just slide across it. As you pull, this will tighten up the ball and add tension to it.

C. Give the loaf a quarter-turn and repeat this tightening step. Proceed in this way until you've gone all the way around the dough ball two or three times. The loaf doesn't need to be super-tight, but you don't want it to be loose, either. You want enough tension so the loaf holds its shape and its gases. If the shaped loaf is too soft, without enough tension, there's less physical structure to hold on to the gases. Some gas will escape, resulting in bread that's smaller and a bit heavier than the ideal.

D. Place your shaped loaf seam-side down in a floured proofing basket. You need to use enough flour so the fully proofed loaf can be removed without it sticking but not so much that you end up with a lot of excess flour on the loaf. A new basket needs more flour than one that is experienced. (See the photos on the facing page.)

Learning a New Skill

Some things just require practice and repetition. Know that you are developing a skill that will improve over time and will be valuable to you for the rest of your life. Assuming you already pay very close attention to the written instructions, you may find it helpful to watch my YouTube channel where you can see my hands in action in each of the steps (just search "Ken Forkish"); I have videos that demonstrate each stage. Look at where and how my hands handle the dough.

Step 6: Proof the Bread

The second rise, called the *proof*, begins right after you have shaped the loaf and put it into its pan or proofing basket. Time and temperature are the two elements that determine how long to let your shaped loaf rise before it's ready to bake. If it takes 1 hour at room temperature, it can take 12 hours or more if held the entire time in the refrigerator. Bake too soon and you get a dense loaf of bread. Wait too long and it can flop over the edges of your pan or over-proof and stick to the proofing basket! If you follow the recipe guidelines for timing and temperature, you should be successful the first time; but pay attention to the rise and the indicators that I give you. Let your oven preheat for 45 minutes or so before baking and it will be ready when you are.

OPEN-PAN LOAVES

The timing on the overnight cold-proofed pan-bread recipes might seem risky in that it feels like too much. The loaves that proof overnight in the refrigerator usually expand more than those that proof in an hour at room temperature. Cold tightens the gluten in the dough, giving it more strength to hold its form while the dough expands—more than room temperature dough. When the magic hour hits in the morning and you are ready to put the loaf into the oven, that's when you want the rise to be at a place you feel it might have gone too far. Pushing up and threatening to flop over the edge of the pan but not quite—that's the perfect point! See the photo on page 50.

The quest is for a loaf that, once in the high heat of the oven, rises high and spreads out too. A slice from one of these loaves will have attractive "ears" at the top where the dough is wider than at the bottom. You'll know when you have it perfect if you try once and it's a bit too much; it's the only way you'll ever

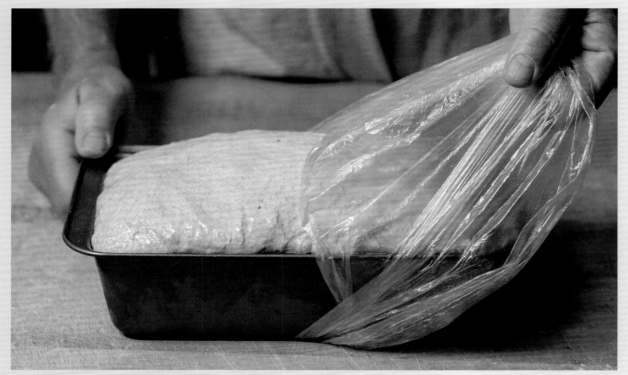

A thin film of water on the shaped loaf lets the bag peel right off.

Perfect proof, ready to bake: two different pans.

EVOLUTIONS IN BREAD

nail what the limit is. This gets to what I find most consuming about baking bread at home; little things like this become a quest. The bread will still be really good if you missed the perfect proof. If it was a little too much, it will flop over the edge and might take some work to pry it off once out of the oven. But sometimes it's a bull's-eye—heck, yeah. So go for the ears, the Goldilocks point in the proofing where the dough is rising above the rim of the pan. When you hit it right, the loaf will rise and spread out a bit at the top during the bake. And getting the maximum expansion will yield the lightest texture too.

I cover the loaf in a plastic bag to keep it from drying out. In my first recipe tests, the risen dough stuck to the plastic bag covering it. Again, the solution is simple: Using your hand, spread a thin film of water over the entire top of the loaf and then place your bread pan in a nonperforated plastic bag, leaving it loose at the top so the dough can expand. Or you could instead cover the loaf loosely with plastic wrap. It will peel off easily if you have applied the film of water.

If you are using the smaller USA Pan (8½ by 4½ by 2¾ inches), the dough should have inflated above the pan rim. It might look like too much! No fear. A little bit of droop over the edges is desirable, and it should look domed in the middle. The bag should peel right off.

LIDDED-PAN LOAVES

This is simple. Let the dough rise inside the pan with the lid in place; seam up or down doesn't matter. When the dough is almost hitting the lid, it's time to bake. If the dough is hitting the lid and you can't slide it open, it's fine. Go ahead and bake it. The lid should stay in place, and the loaf will come out with nice squared edges.

DUTCH-OVEN LOAVES

Whether the loaf proofs at room temperature or overnight in the refrigerator, the goal is to keep it from drying out. Putting the proofing basket into a nonperforated plastic bag (I use grocery store produce bags) is the best way to go. Lacking that, you could cover the top of the proofing basket with tight-fitting plastic wrap. If you fear the dough hitting the plastic wrap and sticking to it, once the loaf is in the basket, use your hand to apply a light film of water across the surface of the dough. If it hits the plastic wrap, the plastic will peel right off.

In *Flour Water Salt Yeast* and in this book's Dutch-oven recipes, I mention the finger-dent test for proofing. It remains the most foolproof method that I know. To do the test, poke the rising loaf with a floured finger, making an indentation about ½ inch deep. If it springs back immediately, the loaf needs more proofing time. If the indentation springs back slowly and incompletely, the loaf is fully proofed and ready to bake. If the indentation doesn't spring back at all, the loaf may be a little past its prime point for baking but not necessarily overproofed. Don't panic! Go ahead and bake, knowing the loaf may collapse a bit when you remove it from its basket or put it into the Dutch oven for baking. (It depends on how over-proofed it actually is—I'm sometimes surprised to find that a loaf I thought overproofed holds its form and bakes up just fine.) It is worth noting that dough mixed with higher protein bread flour has more tolerance for extended proofing before it collapses.

The same-day bread recipes for Dutch-oven baking take a little longer to proof than the pan breads from the same dough—1¼ to 1½ hours total. This is when you need to put the loaves in the oven. The overnight cold-proof recipes will have you shape and place the dough into a basket and put it into the refrigerator overnight. These are excellent breads and my favorite for the timing: I like to bake first thing in the morning. The cold dough will develop more slowly, giving you a window of ideal proofing that lasts for a couple of hours.

Step 7: Preheat

It's important to know your oven. Many home ovens run hotter or cooler than the temperature you set them to. Mine runs about 25°F cooler; so when I set it to 500°F, I actually get 475°F. The temperatures given in the recipes are, of course, the actual temperature the bread should be baked at, so I recommend that you use an oven thermometer. They cost only a few dollars, and using one will ensure that you're baking at the proper temperature, allowing you to follow the suggested baking times with confidence.

OPEN- AND LIDDED-PAN LOAVES
About 45 minutes prior to baking, position a rack in the middle of the oven and preheat the oven to 450°F / 230°C.

DUTCH-OVEN LOAVES
Position a rack in the middle of the oven. If you bake too close to the bottom of the oven, you run the risk of scorching the bottom of the loaf. Put your 4-quart Dutch oven, with the lid, on the middle rack. (There is no need to place the Dutch oven on a pizza stone; it would likely scorch the bottom of your bread.) Preheat the oven to 475°F / 245°C for 45 minutes. The goal is for the Dutch oven to be fully saturated with heat before you place the loaf inside of it.

Heat Shield to Prevent Scorching the Bottom of Your Dutch-Oven Loaf
Home ovens normally heat from the bottom, and that's the hot spot. Sometimes, depending on the oven, baking bread looks good on top but ends up scorched on the bottom. (The Apple-Cider Levain Bread on page 229, with the sugars in the cider, is very susceptible to this.) If this is a problem, here is what you can do:

A. Make sure your Dutch oven is on a middle rack in your oven, as high above the heating element as will fit. Position a rack on the next lowest rung.

B. About 30 minutes into the bake, slide a cast-iron skillet (preferred) or a sheet pan, your "heat shield," on the lower rack directly beneath the Dutch oven. This usually does the trick. If still a problem (sorry!), do this earlier in the bake or refrigerate your heat shield ahead of time.

Step 8: Bake

Baking the bread always feels like a victory lap to me. The house or apartment smells so good, it's like sunshine on a cloudy day.

OPEN-PAN LOAVES
Put your pan into the oven on the center of the middle rack and then turn the temperature to 425°F / 220°C. Set the timer for 30 minutes to check for even baking; if the bread isn't baking evenly, turn the pan 180 degrees. A bake time of 50 minutes has repeatedly been the ideal for all the open-pan bread recipes in my tests, but it's always good to check at around 45 minutes to tune in to the final minutes of the bake until you are confident in your oven and the timeline. The top of the pan loaf bakes to a much darker color than the sides and bottom. If you think it's done when the top is light brown, you'll discover the sides are baked too light, and the loaf may collapse on itself. Bake until the top is dark brown, and the rest of the loaf will be golden colored.

Place loaves into a preheated oven.

Oven spring!

If you have a nonstick bread pan, the loaf should pop right out. But not always, and that's why I recommend giving even nonstick pans a spritz of cooking spray ahead of time. Sometimes the edges of the loaf overlap the sides of smaller bread pans, like the USA Pan, and the loaf becomes a little bit stuck. With oven mitts or kitchen towels protecting your hands, rap the bread pan forcefully on a wooden or other hard surface that won't be damaged. If that doesn't do the trick, grab the edge of the pan with one hand (protected by a folded kitchen towel) and pry out the loaf with your other hand. Sounds kludgy, but if you have a nonstick pan it will come out with some prying. Let the loaf cool on a wire rack, so air can flow around it.

LIDDED-PAN LOAVES

Put your bread pan, shaped loaf inside and lid closed, into the oven on the center of the middle rack and then turn the temperature to 425°F / 220°C. Set the timer for 40 minutes to check for even baking; open the lid and check for color. This is more of a blind bake than the open-pan loaves. A bake time of 50 minutes has repeatedly been the ideal for all the lidded-pan bread recipes in my tests. The dough will rise into the shape of the pan, ideally with squared-off edges. Pop the bread out of the pan immediately after baking. Let the loaf cool on a wire rack, so air can flow around it.

When Is This Bread Ready to Slice?

How long should you wait to cut into your freshly baked loaf? Funny question? Maybe. It all depends on how you slice it. When still warm from the oven, and even several hours later, open-pan loaves are soft. Thicker slices are not much of a problem. A thin slice is about impossible, as the bread needs to be more firm, which comes with time as the loaf loses water content through natural evaporation. When it dries out some (not a lot), its sides set up enough to make slicing it easier. These loaves are moist, so they last longer without going stale. If I want sandwich slices, I wait until the bread is at least a day old and then it works for thin slices for several days after baking, if it lasts that long. And, of course, the better your knife, the more even and cleaner your slices will be.

DUTCH-OVEN LOAVES

I recommend using oven mitts when working with Dutch ovens. Oven mitts go partway up your forearms, providing protection from the high heat of the Dutch oven and its lid. Once a Dutch oven is out of the oven, I find it helpful to put the mitts on the hot lid-handle so I won't absentmindedly pick it up without first putting on a mitt. Take every precaution.

To transfer the dough from the proofing basket to the Dutch oven, carefully invert the proofed loaf onto a floured countertop and give one edge of the basket a firm rap on the counter, hopefully to pop out the whole thing. If the loaf sticks to the edges of the proofing basket, use one hand to delicately release the dough—*and make a mental note that you need to dust the basket with more flour the next time.* Ideally, the weight of the dough should cause it to ease onto the countertop without any assistance. New wicker baskets need more flour than seasoned baskets; the baskets do not need to be cleaned between uses, as they improve with age and use.

If the bread dough clinging to your proof basket continues to be a problem, then your dough is probably too sticky. Perhaps your flour is less absorbent than mine, which means you can cut back the water in the recipe by 20 or 30 grams to compensate. Maybe the dough is fine, but you need to work on how you shape the loaf. Make sure you fold the dry, flour-dusted side of the dough over the sticky interior part when you form the round—and give it some tension as you shape it. Next, very carefully place the loaf in the hot Dutch oven. The dough is already resting on the counter right-side up, so just pick it up and place it in the Dutch oven without flipping it over. Use the broad part of your hands and fingers, not your fingertips, to pick up the loaf and set it in the pot. It's delicate at this stage, and it's best to spread the pressure needed to pick it up across the dough.

Invert the proof basket and give it a firm rap on a floured surface to release the loaf.

With floured hands, pick up the loaf from underneath.

Gently place the loaf into a very hot Dutch oven. Be careful.

Use the mitts to put the lid on the Dutch oven and return it to the center of the middle rack of the preheated oven. Set a timer for 30 minutes to check for even baking; remove the lid, the loaf will be fully risen, there should be one or more attractive splits in the top where the dough expanded, and the crust should be a light brown. Set the timer for another 20 minutes and use that time as a guideline for how long to bake the loaf uncovered. Be sure to check about 5 minutes before the time has elapsed so you're in tune with the loaf's progress. Bake until the loaf is dark brown all around. The raisin-pecan (this pan loaf recipe also makes a terrific Dutch-oven bread) and apple breads will color faster than the other breads in this book because of the added sugars from fruit juices in the dough, so you can shorten the total bake time a bit on these two to compensate.

When the bread is fully baked, remove the Dutch oven from your oven and tilt the pot to turn out. Let the loaf cool on its side (note: on its side is specific to Dutch-oven loaf cooling) or on a wire rack, so air can flow around it, for 20 to 30 minutes, or 1 hour for the rye breads, before slicing. The inside of the loaf continues to bake after it's removed from the oven, and it needs that time to finish. Enjoy the crackling sound of the cooling bread.

Other Variables: Temperature and Season

For most of the recipes in this book, the guidance is to let the dough rise in its dough tub until it reaches $1/2$ to $1/4$ inch below the 2-quart line, or until it is increased in volume about two and a half times. The rise takes longer in a cool room than in a warm room.

The temperature of the dough directly controls the rate of its rise. Warmer temperatures accelerate the metabolic rate of the yeast and other organic components in the dough, which makes it rise faster. Cooler temperatures slow down this activity. The goal in recipe writing is to be able to plan how long the rise will be before moving on to the next step. If time is variable, the amount of rise is not.

The pan-bread recipes that suggest a $3^1/2$-hour rise in my house at 68° to 70°F / 20° to 21°C might be ready in $2^1/2$ to 3 hours in summer. If your house is cooler than mine, it could take 4 hours. The Dutch-oven levain recipes, like my Country Bread EIB-style, complete their rise in my house in 4 hours in the summer but take 5 hours in winter. Be sure to follow the amount of total rise and let that be your ultimate guide for when to remove the dough from its container and make up your loaf.

The same principles apply for the final rise as the dough proofs before baking.

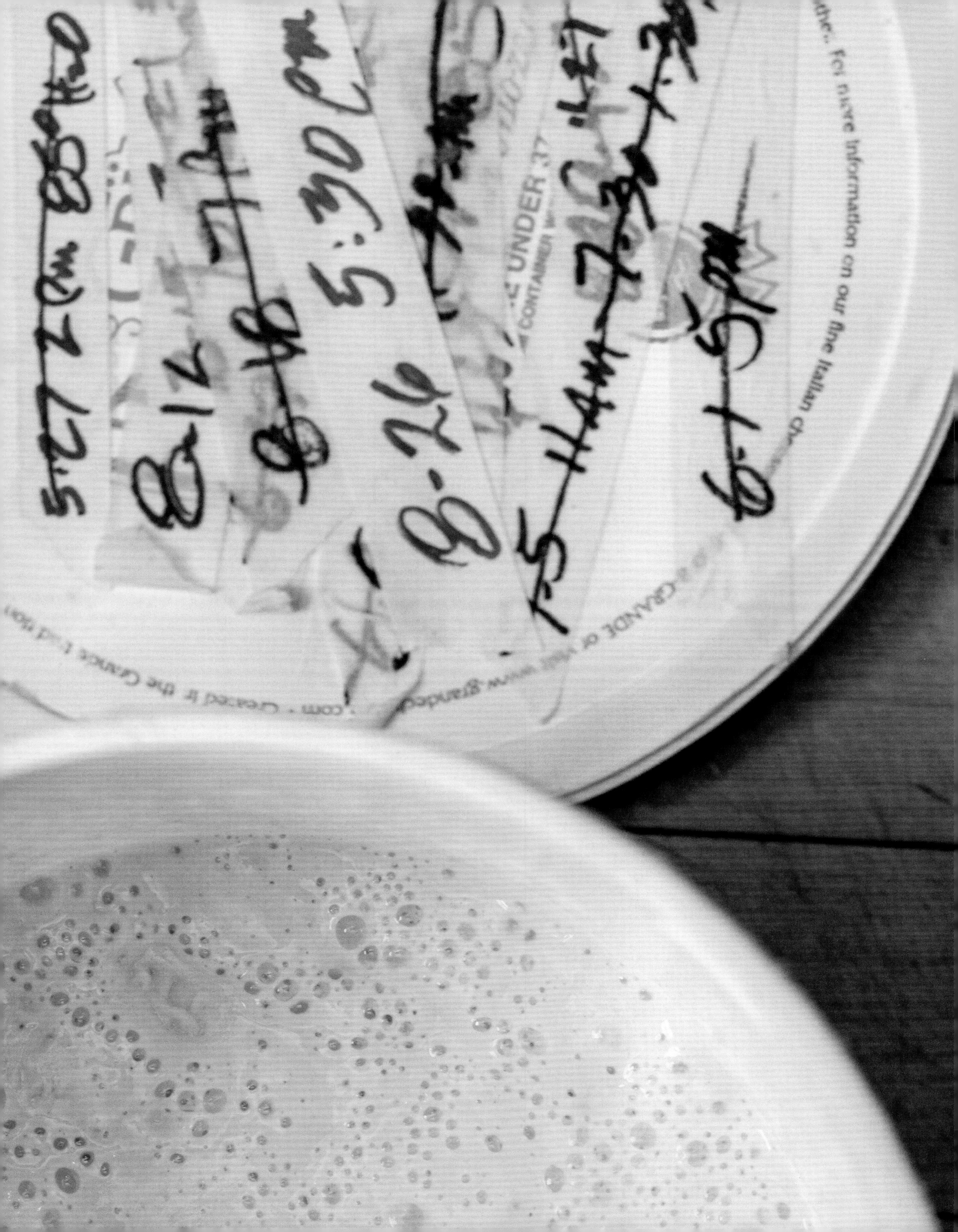

CHAPTER 3
LEVAIN = SOURDOUGH
(A NEW APPROACH)

I have my levain in the fridge at home; it doesn't have a name. The label says "levain" and the date it was last fed. It's a goopy sourdough culture that was made by mixing flour and water. The yeast cells came from the air and from the flour; they were fruitful, and soon the culture contained many billions of yeast cells. It took a week to start it—5 minutes each day, including cleanup. I feed it about once every 7 to 10 days with more flour and water. After its feeding, it sits out 20 to 24 hours—it's lively, gassy, and covered with small bubbles—and then it goes back into the fridge. It's good to use again at this point. The cycle of weekly refresh can go on forever; there are some levains that are decades old.

Store-bought commercial yeast is a monoculture, one specific kind of yeast. A levain culture hosts multiple varieties of naturally occurring yeasts and becomes a specific biome with behavior that depends on the flour you feed it, how much water you put in it, where you live, and at what temperature it is kept. Because of this more complex biology versus commercial yeast, breads made from your levain will have a more complex flavor. They also last longer before going stale.

When I'm ready to make bread with this natural yeast culture, I have two choices. First, I can use it to build a sourdough starter. This starter will leaven the final dough mix all by itself, no commercial yeast needed. You'll read more about this option later, in the chapter on levain breads. Or I could mix a simpler dough that gets its rise from a combination of store-bought yeast and the levain and proceed from there without making up a starter. This makes a long-fermented bread dough with one less step. It has a taste, texture, and character of its own—so good that this became my most-baked style of pan bread at home. Check out the breads under Same-Day Recipes or Overnight Cold-Proof Recipes (these make very good Dutch-oven loaves too).

In *The Elements of Pizza*, I wrote instructions for starting a new levain culture from scratch that used a lot less flour than in *Flour Water Salt Yeast*, and I called it Levain 2.0. It stores in a usable state as a refrigerated culture, as I'm doing in this book. Here, the start-up method for creating a new levain culture from scratch is similar to my pizza version, though this one has steps that make it more suitable for bread baking. It uses considerably less flour than my original levain from *Flour Water Salt Yeast*.

It takes about 650 grams / 1½ pounds flour total to build your levain culture from scratch. That's it!

Natural Culture

Biological processes occur as soon as you mix flour and water together—yeasts that were in the flour and the air are given resources to reproduce. Enzymes in the flour-water dough break down the natural starches in flour into simple sugars that are food for yeast. The yeast reproduce and belch out fermentation gases. Lactic acid bacteria do their own fermenting. Lots of good things happen.

Terms

There are many words for a natural levain, but they all basically mean the same thing. This is how I distinguish them.

Levain—This is the French word for *sourdough*: a wild-yeast leavening dough that is made up from many feedings of flour and water. A previous generation of bakers might have called it a *mother*, or *chef* if in France. It is the seed culture for recipe-specific starters that are built from it. In this book, it is also used as a flavoring element that goes straight into dough mixes that are primarily fermented from commercial (store-bought) yeast.

Sourdough—I use the words *levain* and *sourdough* interchangeably for readability. I don't want my breads to taste sour, so, historically, I have preferred to use the French word *levain* instead, but they are the same thing. I use the word *sourdough* more often in this book than I've done before, because I think it's a more familiar term to many readers.

Starter—This is a recipe-specific culture that leavens the dough. The term *starter* is used generically for both natural levain starters, as it is here, and for yeasted starters, like a poolish or biga. In this book's levain bread recipes, the starter is made with a small amount of the refrigerated levain culture mixed with flour and water, and it is fed three times to build up its strength sufficiently to make the dough rise and impart good, balanced flavors and acidity.

The design of this book's sourdough recipes has you create a levain culture that you store in the refrigerator, pluck from as needed, and refresh roughly once a week, or sooner if you are running low. I want a consistent fermentation of the levain at its weekly feeding so I get consistent leavening power, flavors that are in harmony, and a predictable timeline for the fermentation of the dough that is ultimately made from the culture. When it's time for a refresh, you may have a little more remaining in your levain container than what is needed for its weekly feeding. You can either toss the extra (it's not going to be much) or you can use it to begin a new starter or dough—it's a good excuse to keep baking!

For those who have used the levain methods and recipes in *Flour Water Salt Yeast*, you'll see a progression in my thinking on home baking from then to now, ten years later. There was plenty of development in our practices at my bakeries during this span too. The *Flour Water Salt Yeast* methods work consistently and with excellent results. I stand behind them. However, they do use more flour than is necessary to make one loaf of sourdough bread.

One way of looking at what's different in this book's levain method versus the method that I wrote up in *Flour Water Salt Yeast* is that in my first book, I used the same process that we use at my bakeries. We maintain a single levain (it can build up to as much as 36 kilograms for our mixes). We feed that culture three times a day—twice in the early morning to build it up to be ripe for the day's dough mixes and then, once it's mostly used up, we feed it again to get it ready for the next morning's series of feedings.

It never stops at a bakery; the levain cycle is always in a state of change. We use that levain when it is at a very particular stage in its evolution. We're looking for that just-ripe point where it has the leavening power to ferment the dough. It's also going to impart a balanced complexity of fermented flavors without being too sour. The sour would come if there was an excess of fermentation in the levain itself, like if we were to wait longer to mix dough from it. Each day, we make enough levain to meet the needs of our dough mixes that use it, and there's a little bit left over. When it is time to feed our levain again, we start with just a small amount of culture to build up to 36 kilograms of levain 20 hours later—it's hungry and it grows fast! And then the next day we start over.

For this book, I've economized a bit on flour, and I can show you a new way to do it. Here, I use a levain that stays stable in refrigerated storage and it is the seed that builds a starter for each recipe. The starter takes a while to wake up and build its strength. The refresh feedings you'll see in the recipes add to the culture's leavening power and prevent too much acidity from developing.

The next section shows you how to start a levain culture. It then gives you a long-form description of how it works, how to use it in the recipes, and, finally, how to maintain it.

How to Start Your Own Levain in Seven Days

It takes almost no time to create your own levain culture that you can then use to make bread (and pizza) for years to come. Less than 5 minutes a day for 7 days and you're there. Follow that with feedings every week, or when you run low, and you can keep it going for as long as you want. Store it in the fridge.

The first thing you need is a container big enough to handle the final version of this culture and shaped to make it easy to mix flour and water in it by hand. Tall and narrow is awkward; wide is good. A rounded, 2-quart see-through container with a matching lid

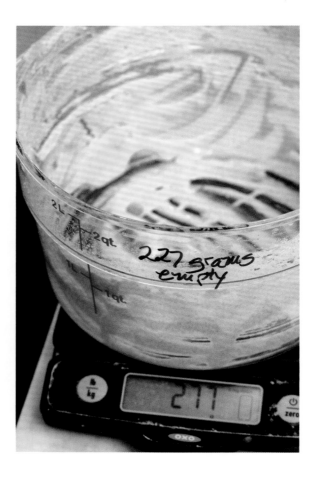

does the trick. Weigh the empty container without the lid and write down that weight on the container. Masking tape and a Sharpie are good for this. You'll need to know the container weight later when you want to know how much culture remains in the container—for example, when I ask you to remove all but 50 grams / ¼ cup of the culture.

You will also need whole-wheat flour and white flour to establish your levain, the beating heart and source of leavening for your future sourdough breads. The active organic elements in wheat flour contribute to the creation of a fertile levain culture that's home to billions and billions of yeast cells that will give your bread dough lift and flavor.

There are two stages here: creation of the culture and then maintenance and rebuild feedings. First, it will be 7 days of once-a-day feedings of small amounts of flour and water to create a new levain culture.

It will take fewer than 5 minutes a day, including cleanup. The result of this start-up stage is the creation of a culture of mature levain that will be kept in a refrigerator in a usable state for an extended period of time with no maintenance. You will then pluck 50 to 100 grams / ¼ to ½ cup of this to build a starter or to mix into your bread dough any time you want. The second stage—care and feeding—can last forever, really. Periodic feeding of the levain will keep it alive and replenish the supply after you have been using it.

Try to do the daily mixes of flour and water for this start-up phase at roughly the same time each day, so there is about a full day of development before you move on to the next mix. (Evenings were most convenient for me.) This method uses small amounts of flour, but it works! To start your levain, you'll need the following:

- Container with matching lid. A 2-quart tub is a good size. (If you need to order one, you can start with a small mixing bowl and cover it with plastic wrap, then transfer the culture partway when your 2-quart tub arrives.)
- Digital probe thermometer
- 250 grams / 1¾ cups + 1¾ tsp whole-wheat flour
- 400 grams / 2¾ cups + 2 tsp white flour (all-purpose or bread flour is fine)
- Water

I chose to offer you both metric gram weight and volume measurements in this levain creation process because if the scale you ordered is on backorder you can make approximations with cups and still get a good levain started! On Day 5, I ask you to remove and toss all but 100 grams / ½ cup of the levain you have been creating. You'll have to guess at what ½ cup of culture remaining looks like in

your container. Just guess, it'll be fine. Don't try to empty the container, measure out ½ cup of the culture and pour it back in. It's an unnecessary, messy hassle. The culture sticks to the container and to the cup, and you'll never get it right. If you have a scale, it's simple: subtract the weight of the empty container from the weight of the container with stuff in it. That's why I have you write down the container weight ahead of time. On Day 6 and in the levain maintenance feedings, I ask you to remove and toss all but 50 grams / ¼ cup of the levain. We have a photo of 50 grams culture remaining in the tub on the facing page to show what it should look like.

Day 1

Use a size and shape of container that's compatible with your refrigerator (for Day 8 and beyond) and the amount of space you will need to carve out for it. By hand, mix 50 grams / ⅓ cup + 1¼ tsp whole-wheat flour with 50 grams / 3 Tbsp + 1 tsp (95° to 100°F /35° to 38°C) water. Let it sit out with the lid off for an hour or two, then put the lid on it. Leave it out at room temperature—68° to 70°F / 20° to 21°C is fine—overnight.

Day 2 *(roughly 24 hours later)*

Add 50 grams / ⅓ cup + 1¼ tsp whole-wheat flour and 50 grams /3 Tbsp + 1 tsp (95° to 100°F / 35° to 38°C) water to what you made yesterday and mix by hand. Let it sit out with the lid off for an hour or two, then put the lid on it. Do not refrigerate.

Day 3 *(roughly 24 hours later)*

Two days after you started, the new culture should be gassy and alive! Add 50 grams / ⅓ cup + 1¼ tsp whole-wheat flour and 50 grams / 3 Tbsp + 1 tsp (95° to 100°F / 35° to 38°C) water and mix by hand. Put the lid on it. Do not refrigerate.

Day 4 *(roughly 24 hours later)*

Throw away *none* of the bubbly goop. Add 100 grams / ½ cup + 3 Tbsp + 1¼ tsp whole-wheat flour and 100 grams / ¼ cup + 2 Tbsp + 2 tsp (95° to 100°F / 35° to 38°C) water and mix by hand. Put the lid on it. Do not refrigerate. If your culture is not showing any signs of life before its feeding, something's wrong. You should stop, throw it away, and try again with a different brand of whole-wheat flour.

Day 5 *(roughly 24 hours later)*

You should see and feel the carbonated, alcoholic web of lively culture that has been built up so far. Now you will switch to white flour. Please reference the empty weight of your container that you wrote down before you started. This part is a little messy, so keep a kitchen towel nearby, use a wet hand, and have your scale right there. Stand next to the trash can and dump the mixture until 100 grams / ½ cup remains. Add 100 grams / ¼ cup + 2 Tbsp + 2 tsp (85°F / 29°C) water and 100 grams / ½ cup + 3 Tbsp + 1¼ tsp white flour. Mix by hand. Put the lid on it and let it sit out overnight.

To this point, the feedings with whole-wheat flour have built up the population of yeast and lactic acid bacteria in the culture and its support-ing biome. There are more flora and nutritive elements from the wheat germ and bran that are in whole-wheat flour than in white flour. I always use whole-grain flour to start a levain culture for this reason. This step begins the conversion to a white-flour levain and uses cooler water in the mix. This will allow the levain to build and normalize its permanent flour makeup and migrate to being less acidic (a by-product of the fermentation), and that's why I have you throw away all but 100 grams / ½ cup of it at this step. This new culture you are creating should now be very gassy and fragrant. You should smell its leathery aromas and get an aromatic hint of its acidity too.

Day 6, morning

Remove all but 50 grams / ¼ cup of culture, toss the rest, and add 100 grams / ½ cup + 3 Tbsp + 1¼ tsp white flour and 100 grams / ¼ cup + 2 Tbsp + 2 tsp (80°F / 27°C) water. Mix by hand. Cover and let it sit out for 24 hours.

Day 7, morning

The culture you've spent a week building is ready now to make up your long-term levain that will be kept in the refrigerator and restored every 7 to 10 days, or as necessary to meet your baking needs and to keep it in good condition. Prior to this feeding, it should be super-gassy and seem fully alive, fizzy almost with a little bit of froth on the top. When you reach your hand into it to discard the excess, it should feel light and airy, with a delicate webbing. It should also have a mellow, complex, lactic-alcohol smell of fermentation with a hint of background acidity.

Remove all but 50 grams / ¼ cup of culture and add 200 grams / 1¼ cups + 2 Tbsp + 2½ tsp white flour and 200 grams / ¾ cup + 1 Tbsp + 1 tsp (80°F / 27°C) water. Mix by hand, then cover. Let it sit out for about 24 hours and then refrigerate. This is your levain. It will now be usable for any of the recipes in this book.

Why a White-Flour Levain?

At my bakeries, I have used levain cultures that have a blend of white flour and whole-wheat flour; in *Flour Water Salt Yeast*, the levain is 80 percent white flour and 20 percent whole-wheat flour. The flavors from these are earthy and good. I also like the flavor from an all-white-flour levain, it is different and nice to show you another way to do it. The white-flour levain gives a little bit more lactic and fruity flavors and takes longer to develop sour flavors. Whole-wheat flour leads to a faster fermentation compared with white-flour cultures, and acetic acid is a by-product of an over-fermented dough.

Fifty grams levain remain in the bucket.

Feed with equal amounts of flour and water.

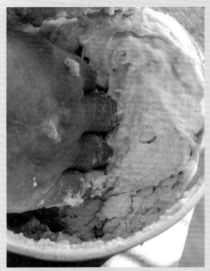

Mix by hand and let sit out 20 to 24 hours.

Levain Maintenance Feedings

Your freshly mixed levain weighs 450 grams. Each recipe in this book uses either 50 grams / ¼ cup or 100 grams / ½ cup of this culture. When it's time to refresh the culture, use the same container as its permanent home. Don't wash out the container; just remove all but 50 grams / ¼ cup of what is left in there, add more flour and water, and mix by hand.

Refresh feeding, enough for four loaves of pan bread in the next 7 to 10 days:

- 50 grams / ¼ cup retained culture
- 200 grams / 1¼ cups + 2 Tbsp + 2½ tsp white flour (bread flour or all-purpose flour is fine)
- 200 grams / ¾ cup + 1 Tbsp + 1 tsp (75°F / 24°C in summer, 85°F / 29°C in winter) water

Mix by hand until all the elements are combined. Cover and let it sit out at room temperature for 20 to 24 hours, then refrigerate.

If you want more on hand than the 450 grams that each refresh yields, you can build up a bigger levain. Here's how:

- 50 grams / ¼ cup retained culture
- 400 grams / 2¾ cups + 2 tsp white flour
- 400 grams / 1½ cups + 2 Tbsp + 2 tsp (75°F / 24°C in summer, 85°F / 29°C in winter) water

Mix by hand until all the elements are combined. Cover and let it sit out at room temperature for 20 to 24 hours, then refrigerate. The retained culture amount does not need to increase with the larger amounts of flour and water because the yeast replication at the beginning of the process happens fast at warm temperatures and it starts to ferment quickly.

Again, your room temperature is relevant. If your levain is sitting out at, say, 65°F / 18°C overnight, a full 24 hours is good before refrigerating it. But if your room temperature is 80°F / 27°C, you'll reach that same point of maturity in the culture much faster—in about 12 hours. Eventually, you'll figure it out. Not enough time will result in bread doughs that take too long to rise and don't ever quite reach their potential volume. Too much time will over-ferment the culture and you'll get more sour flavors.

When to feed it? As the days pass with the culture in the refrigerator (at about 37°F / 3°C), the community of yeasts will start to die off without new nutrients, and it will lose its potency. Even though it's cold in there, your culture does evolve, though slowly. I don't have a magic formula of, say, every 7 days or every 10 days, but it's in that zone. If you forget it for a few weeks, you will be able to restore it. But the point is for you to have a culture at hand that you can use whenever you want and be confident in its performance. Use it frequently and you will need to refresh the culture just to have more at hand.

The rate at which you feed your levain can be more frequent if you bake often. It could be daily, every 3 days—it doesn't matter. But it'll start to change for the not-so-awesome if you let it go a couple weeks without feeding. I have rescued some that I thought were long gone, but it took a couple days of maintenance feedings to build them back up to something I'd want to bake with. And you want to consider leavening performance and how it makes your bread taste too! Plenty of sourdough cultures will make the dough rise but don't provide the balanced flavor set that I'm looking for in my breads. And that was my biggest challenge in using this book's low-waste approach—early attempts didn't give enough lift, and later attempts gave the lift but the flavor was too sour. It took some refinement to get to a process for you to use that will make bread I'd be happy with.

Levain Fermentation

First off, it's pretty cool how little culture you need to seed the next feeding. To reiterate, my base level in this book is to refresh the levain with 50 grams of retained culture and 200 grams flour plus 200 grams water, then you leave it out for 20 to 24 hours (overnight is not enough, although it might look like it is) and it's bubbly and ready for action and a return to life in the refrigerator. If you need to build up more, with 400 grams flour and water, you still need only 50 grams of retained culture, and it will build up to its mature point in almost same amount of time.

To help you understand what's going on, imagine what's at work on the cellular level. Yeast cells duplicate fast, but instead of birthing brand-new yeast cells one at a time, each one grows buds—as many as a dozen or so. In short order, each of those buds grows into its own yeast cell, same as the one it came from—and they bud, and those bud, and so on. So, you can see how, when the environment is right, your entry number of yeast cells will increase to a big number very quickly. All they need is food, water, oxygen, and a nice temperature (yeast cells' metabolic rate increases with temperature, up to about 114°F / 46°C; higher temps will kill them off). Their food is simple sugars derived from the starch in flour (complex carbs in flour are broken down into simple sugars—glucose, primarily—by the enzyme known as amylase, which, lucky for us, is naturally occurring in wheat and rye flour).

After a certain point, the population of yeasts will shift from mostly replicating to mostly fermenting. Yeast will replicate as long as there is oxygen in their environment, and once the environment becomes anaerobic (without oxygen), their activity converts to fermentation: they eat sugars and output CO_2 gas and ethanol. But it's not a hard-stop shift from one activity to the next in bread dough. There's usually some of each activity—reproduction and fermentation—that's going on simultaneously.

My goal is for the levain culture to build up a large yeast population without getting too much fermentation activity early in the process—an excess of fermentation will produce acetic acids, the source of "sour" in sourdough. The best way to get to my desired mellow levain is to start with a very small amount of culture and feed it with good-quality flour and warm water.

Starter is ready; lid on 2-quart container with times of each feeding. The third feeding used 95°F / 35°C water.

How to Mix Starters for the Dutch-Oven Levain Bread Recipes

The Dutch-oven levain bread recipes take 2 days of build-up so that the starter has enough leavening power to give the dough a good rise. The starters are simple mixes by hand that begin with 50 grams of levain from the refrigerator and a small amount of flour and water. Each mix takes just a couple of minutes. The starter gets two feedings on Day 1 and a third feeding on the morning of Day 2. Then, 7 or 8 hours later, the final dough is mixed.

The timing and the feedings are also designed to make the bread taste good. I want to taste the fermented flavors without the bread being sour. Texturally, a complete fermentation from this culture will show a variety of open holes throughout the inside of the bread, with no dense crumb. If you have good-quality flour and you nail it with the dough using this method, the flavor and texture of your bread are going to be awesome.

It takes a long time for the yeast from the cold culture to wake up and turn into something that is once again active. I did try many variations of a single-feed starter, as I did for pizza dough in *The Elements of Pizza*, but bread dough needs a greater rise than pizza dough. Other levain timing and feeding schemes that I tried, which seemed easier and more convenient, tasted strongly sour and took too long to rise. This is the method that works.

There will be some extra starter when you get to the third feed, so what to do with it? Make two batches of bread dough. Or I have a delicious sourdough pizza dough recipe on page 237. Or you could blend some of it into a pancake batter, make muffins or brownies, and on and on.

When Is the Starter Ready for the Dough?

In my testing, about 7 hours after feeding the Day 2 starter in the morning, I start to see the first bubbles forming, but the starter is not fully covered—it's more like the beginning, and there will be maybe a dozen or so bubbles on top at this point. It's relevant to know when you are at this stage because about an hour later is when the starter will be at its first usable point.

At the earliest time that the starter looks alive and gassy, often with some bubbles popping, it's ready, and at this point it will give you the mellowest flavors. This is when you mix the final dough for any of the levain bread recipes. The starter is viable for the next several hours; yet with more time, it will yield more sour flavors.

Overall Recipe Timing

I like to time everything so my levain doughs are mixed in the late afternoon from a starter mixed that morning. For all the levain recipes except the Apple-Cider Levain Bread, if you mix the Day 2 starter at 8 a.m., the dough would be mixed 7 or 8 hours later. Five hours after that, at 8 p.m. or 9 p.m., it should be fully risen (up to about ½ inch below the 2-quart line in a dough tub with measurements marked on the side) and then it's time to make up the loaf. Refrigerate the loaf overnight and bake it the next morning or early afternoon.

The Apple-Cider Levain Bread recipe has its own schedule that works with an overnight first rise. The loaf is made up first thing in the morning and you will bake it 3½ to 4 hours later.

Cold Storage

When you won't be baking for a few weeks or more, you'll need a storage routine to hold the levain in a kind of suspension until you are ready to bring it back. I've held cultures in my refrigerator for a couple of months and then successfully restored them. There are many methods. Here's what works for me.

Remove 200 grams / 1 cup of the levain (toss the rest and clean your levain tub for later use), place in a large bowl, and mix it by hand with 100 grams / ½ cup + 3 Tbsp + 1¼ tsp white flour and 35 grams / 2 Tbsp + 1 tsp cold water to form a stiff dough. Put it into an airtight container (like a 1-quart vessel with a matching lid or a plastic bag) and cover with another 100 grams / ⅔ cup + 1 Tbsp + 1¼ tsp white flour. Store in the refrigerator.

To restore a levain from cold storage:

Day 1, morning Remove the excess flour from the culture. In a fresh 2-quart container or a big bowl, combine half of the culture, 200 grams / 1¼ cups + 2 Tbsp + 2½ tsp white flour, and 235 grams / 1 cup + 2 tsp (95°F / 35°C) water. Mix by hand, cover, and let it sit at room temperature for 24 hours.

Day 2, morning The culture should be showing signs of life. Remove all but 100 grams / ½ cup and add 100 grams / ½ cup + 3 Tbsp + 1¼ tsp white flour and 100 grams / ¼ cup + 2 Tbsp + 2 tsp (95°F / 35°C) water. Mix by hand, cover, and let it sit at room temperature for 12 hours.

Day 2, evening The culture should look lively and full of bubbles. Remove all but 50 grams / ¼ cup and add 200 grams / 1¼ cups + 2 Tbsp + 2½ tsp white flour and 200 grams / ¾ cup + 1 Tbsp + 1 tsp (85°F / 29°C) water. Mix by hand, cover, and let it sit at room temperature for 20 to 24 hours.

Day 3, evening Your levain should now be ready for use. You can return it to the refrigerator and go back to your weekly refresh schedule.

PART II
RECIPES

A GUIDE TO THE RECIPES

The recipes in this book feature either a particular flour blend, with einkorn, rye, and heritage wheat options among them, or creative breads with nuts, beer, butter, corn, black rice flour, apple-cider levain, and other additions. They are organized into four broad categories by schedule. The Same-Day Recipes work on a six-hour start-to-finish timeline. Shokupan, or Japanese Milk Bread, and Brioche work well on a same-day timeline, too. They are enriched with milk, butter, eggs (brioche only), and sugar and use a stand mixer, so they have their own brief section. If you want to bake first thing in the morning, try the Overnight Cold-Proof Recipes that you start around 5 p.m. or 6 p.m. You make up a loaf and refrigerate it overnight to be baked in the morning. The Dutch-Oven Levain Recipes work on the same schedules as the hybrid levain breads do in *Flour Water Salt Yeast*: all but one mix the final dough in the afternoon, then the shaped loaf gets a cold overnight proof and is baked the next morning or early afternoon. The Apple-Cider Levain Bread recipe is set up with an overnight first rise, and the bread is baked around lunchtime.

Many of the recipes were written to make bread baked in an open loaf pan, yet they can also bake as crusty, round Dutch-oven loaves for a completely different bread from the same dough. Then there are just a few recipes designed as rectangular loaves baked inside lidded pans, but most of the open-pan loaf recipes can also be baked in a lidded pan for a different style of pan bread.

The tables on the next pages give you a quick reference for the organization of the recipes by their schedule, and indicate the primary baking vessel for which the recipe was intended—pan or Dutch oven—though many of the recipes work equally well in either vessel.

First-Timer Recipes

Start with The Standard loaf (see page 81) or the White Bread recipe (see page 87) on its "same-day" schedule. These are the simplest recipes, easy to make, and once you have success with them, you should have the confidence to try the other same-day pan breads. Be sure to read the Methods & Techniques chapter so you can see how it's done. In your first attempts, you can keep things simple and not fuss too much. The bread should still taste great even if it doesn't look perfect. Your loaf should be baked and out of the oven about 6 hours after you start. The rest of the recipes are within the reach of any home baker. I give you all the detail you need to be successful. Please try any one that makes you want to bake!

Same-Day Breads	Primary Vessel	Also Works In
The Standard (page 81)	Open pan	Lidded pan, Dutch oven
White Bread (page 87)	Open pan	Lidded pan, Dutch oven
50% Emmer or Einkorn Bread (page 93)	Open pan	Lidded pan, Dutch oven
50% Rye Bread (page 99)	Open pan	Lidded pan, Dutch oven
Butter Bread (page 105)	Open pan	Lidded pan, Dutch oven
Black Bread (page 111)	Lidded pan	Open pan, Dutch oven
Corn (Flour) Bread (page 117)	Open pan	Dutch oven
Raisin-Pecan Bread (page 125)	Open pan	Lidded pan, Dutch oven
Hazelnut Bread (page 131)	Open pan	Lidded pan, Dutch oven
Multigrain Bread (page 137)	Open pan	Dutch oven

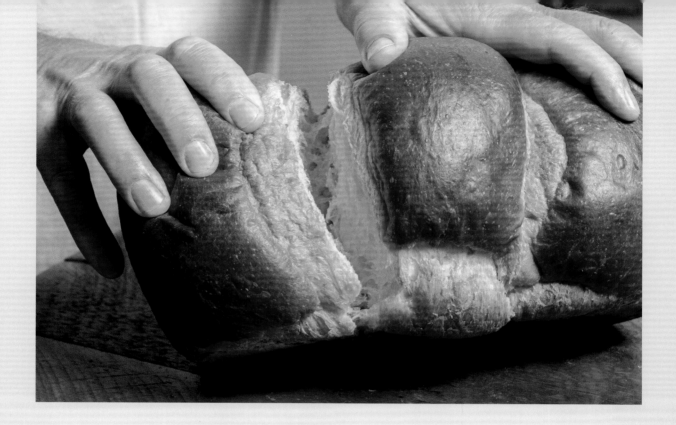

CHAPTER 4
SAME-DAY RECIPES

You can make these same-day breads from start to finish in about 6 hours. And you can do it with or without the recommended levain. But if you commit a small amount of time, just a few minutes each day for a week, to build up a sourdough of your own, you can add this special ingredient. That's when *simple* becomes *really good*. Many of the recipes here tell you the levain is an optional ingredient; it is. But the bread will taste better when you use it. In my side-by-side tests, the bread made with this small amount of levain—100 grams per loaf—had flavors that I can only describe as "warmer" and a little more complex than the straight dough with no added culture.

The first four recipes vary the flour blend, using white flour, whole-wheat flour, rye flour, and emmer or einkorn heritage-grain flour. Then, the next recipes use added ingredients to make Butter Bread, for example, or Hazelnut Bread that has hazelnut meal in it. The Black Bread recipe is made with black rice flour and stout beer; the Raisin-Pecan Bread has tea-soaked raisins, with the soaking liquid added to the dough. Corn (Flour) Bread tastes like corn! The Multigrain Bread recipe uses the grain-soaking liquid in the dough and is an upgraded, simple alternative to supermarket brands—just read their ingredients labels.

These doughs can all be mixed by hand in the dough tub they will rise in. There is minimal cleanup required. The one exception is the dough for Butter Bread. That dough is initially mixed by hand, but then it goes into a stand mixer to blend in cubes of cold butter.

THE STANDARD

Open pan, lidded pan,
or Dutch oven

My friend John McCreary made a few loaves of this and gifted one to another friend who liked it so much that he asked what the secret ingredient was. The special sauce is the bit of levain, which is optional but recommended. You can make this bread without it, but you will be rewarded if you include it.

This bread is not flashy, yet it's the one that I continued to make from the beginning to the end of my recipe testing for this book. It's easy to execute, tastes great, and lasts for about 5 days without going stale. If you want two loaves instead of one, just double the recipe and use a 12-quart dough tub, or equivalent big bowl, to hand mix and ferment the dough. It's also called The Standard because it is easy for this dough to become a standard Dutch-oven bread in your repertoire.

This recipe has more yeast and a slightly shortened fermentation time compared with the doughs in *Flour Water Salt Yeast*. I want pan breads to have more "push" and to rise dramatically above the rim so you will end up with a light and airy crumb. The added yeast gives a more aggressive rise, and the gas it produces gives the dough some extra resilience, too, but it's not so much that it will make the bread taste yeasty.

Using the levain culture in this recipe won't have much impact on the speed of the dough's rise: I tested side-by-side batches with and without it, and they both rose to about the same height on the same timeline. This is my go-to morning toast bread, and it works for any sandwich, croutons, a cheesy French toast, and more.

THIS RECIPE MAKES 1 PAN LOAF OF ABOUT 2 POUNDS.

First rise

3 to 3½ hours at 70°F / 21°C room temperature.
Faster if warmer, slower if cooler.

Proof time

About 1 hour at 70°F / 21°C room temperature.

Bake

Preheat to 450°F / 230°C for 45 minutes,
bake at 425°F / 220°C for about 50 minutes.

Sample schedule

Begin at 9:30 a.m., finish mixing at 10 a.m.,
shape into a loaf at 1:30 p.m., and bake at 2:30 p.m.

Pro Tip: Try using a heritage wheat variety, like Rouge de Bordeaux or Red Fife,
as your whole-wheat flour in this recipe.

Ingredient	Quantity	Baker's Percentage
White bread flour	400 g / 2¾ cups + 2 tsp	80%
Whole-wheat flour	100 g / ⅔ cup + 1 Tbsp + 1¼ tsp	20%
Water (90° to 95°F / 32° to 35°C)	390 g / 1½ cups + 2 Tbsp	78%
Fine sea salt	11 g / 2¼ tsp	2.2%
Instant dried yeast	3 g / 1 tsp	0.6%
Levain (optional)	100 g / ½ cup	9% of total flour (if used)

1. Autolyse

Measure 390 grams (90° to 95°F / 32° to 35°C) water into a 6-quart round tub or similar container. If you have a levain, add 100 grams from the refrigerator—you can weigh it directly into the dough tub with its water. Stir a bit with your fingers to loosen up the culture. Add 400 grams white bread flour and 100 grams whole-wheat flour. Mix it by hand until all is incorporated.

Sprinkle 11 grams fine sea salt evenly across the top of the autolyse dough. Then sprinkle 3 grams instant dried yeast on top of that. Let them rest there, where they will partially dissolve. Don't freak out about the salt and yeast being in contact. It's no worry.

Cover and let rest for 15 to 20 minutes.

2. Mix

Mix by hand, wetting your working hand before mixing so the dough doesn't stick to you. Reach underneath the dough and grab about one-fourth of it. Gently stretch this section and fold it over the top to the other side of the dough. Repeat three more times with the remaining dough until the salt and yeast are fully enclosed.

Use the pincer method to fully integrate the ingredients. Make five or six pincer cuts across the entire mass of dough. Then fold the dough over itself a few times. Repeat, alternately cutting and folding, until all the ingredients are fully integrated. Let the dough rest for a few minutes, then fold for another 30 seconds or until the dough tightens up. The whole process should take about 5 minutes. The target dough temperature at the end of the mix is about 75°F / 24°C. Cover the tub and let the dough rise until the next fold.

3. Fold & First Rise

This dough needs two folds (see page 41). It's easiest to apply the folds during the first hour after mixing the dough. Apply the first fold about 10 minutes after mixing and the second when you see the dough spread out in the tub. If need be, it's okay to fold later; just be sure to leave it alone for the last hour of rising.

When the dough is two and a half to three times its original volume, 3 to 3½ hours after the mix, it's ready to be made up into a loaf and put into its pan. If you are using a 6-quart dough tub, the ideal point is when the edge of the dough has reached just shy (about ¼ inch) of the 2-quart line on the side of the tub, and the dough will be domed—not flattened, not collapsed. If it reaches the 2-quart line on your dough tub, that's fine too. It'll be best if you don't let it go beyond that, as you want to preserve what's left of the rise for the next stage, in the pan. If the room is cool and the dough is taking longer, let it continue to rise until it reaches this amount of volume expansion. If you're not using a marked dough tub, you'll have to eyeball it. Use your best judgment.

4. Remove the Dough from Its Tub

Lightly flour a work surface about 12 inches wide. Flour your hands and sprinkle a bit of flour around the edges of the tub. Tip the tub slightly and then gently work your floured free hand beneath the dough to loosen it from the bottom of the tub. Then turn the tub on its side and ease the dough onto the work surface without pulling or tearing it.

Even if your bread pan is nonstick, you might want to give it a light spritz of cooking spray. Nonstick pans are sometimes not 100 percent nonstick if they have been used a lot.

5. Shape

With floured hands, pick up the dough and ease it back onto the work surface in a somewhat even, rectangular shape. You will stretch and fold this slack dough into something equal to the width of your bread pan.

Following the shaping instructions on pages 43 to 44, with two floured hands, stretch the dough, simultaneously pulling it right and left (just spread your hands both ways at the same time to stretch out the dough) until it resists—two to three times its original width—and then fold the ends back over each other, creating a "packet" the width of your baking pan.

Brush off any loose flour from the top of the dough and do a roll-up motion from the bottom up or from top to bottom to form a tube of dough that's about the same width as your baking pan. Place the dough seam-up into the pan. The seam is usually visible; it's the part of the rolled-up dough where the outer edges have joined to enclose the interior parts of the newly shaped loaf.

Don't stress this. It takes repeated efforts to learn the hand skills to shape sticky, slack bread dough. The pan does much of the work for you, so if all you can manage is to get the dough into the pan, you are not a failure. It'll work fine. Dough bits will stick to your fingers; with time, you will get used to it. My trick is to always grab the dough by its driest outside and flour-covered bottom parts that aren't so sticky. Just avoid leaving any loose flour inside the dough before you roll it up into the pan shape.

6. Proof

Use your hand to apply a light film of water across the entire top surface of the dough after it's in its pan. Then place your bread pan in a nonperforated plastic bag, but do not make it tight at the top. Leave plenty of room for the dough to expand, a few inches, and tuck the bag under the pan. It doesn't need to be airtight. The point of the bag is to keep the dough from drying out during the next hour of proof time.

With my usual bread pan (8½ by 4½ by 2¾ inches), I like to see the dough rising a bit above the rim of the pan before baking, but you can't let it go too far above or it will collapse over the edge. If your pan is larger, the dough likely won't rise above its rim. See photos of perfect proofing on page 50.

Plan on baking the loaf about an hour after it is shaped, assuming a room temperature of about 70°F / 21°C. If your kitchen is warmer, it will be optimally proofed earlier.

7. Preheat

About 45 minutes prior to baking, position a rack in the middle of the oven and preheat the oven to 450°F / 230°C.

8. Bake

Remove the pan from the plastic bag and place it on the center of the oven rack. Turn down the heat to 425°F / 220°C and bake. After 30 minutes, check for even baking (give the pan a turn if the baking is uneven) and bake for another 20 minutes. Because this dough has more water than traditional pan loaves, it needs a longer time than you might think to bake the inside fully and to color the sides and give them enough strength to avoid post-bake collapse.

After 50 minutes, the top of the loaf should be darkly colored. The sides and bottom should not be as dark as the top.

Remove the pan with oven mitts or thick kitchen towels and carefully tilt it to turn the loaf out. If a hard rap on the counter doesn't free the loaf, use a folded kitchen towel to firmly grab one edge of the pan with one hand and use your other hand to pry the loaf out. (Use more cooking spray next time.) Let the loaf cool on a rack, so air can circulate around it, for at least 30 minutes before slicing; 1 hour is better.

WHITE BREAD

Open pan, lidded pan, or Dutch oven

Bread you make at home doesn't have to be complicated to be good. This loaf and The Standard (page 81) introduce you to artisan pan bread that's perfect for sandwiches and toast. And you can also make this recipe as a beautiful, rustic Dutch-oven loaf just by changing the vessel you bake it in.

This bread should be out of the oven about 6 hours after you begin, yet the active time is, maybe, 15 or 20 minutes of effort once you've done it a couple times. If you want fresh bread to bake in the morning, you can do an overnight cold-proof version of this bread (see instructions on page 150). Either way is delicious, and when compared with a packaged, sliced supermarket loaf designed for extended shelf life, well, no comparison really. (Check the ingredients list on that supermarket loaf.)

When I was growing up, my mom would sometimes make sloppy joes, and if we didn't have burger buns, we'd use soft sliced white bread instead. My adult self loves this for a Southern tomato sandwich with Duke's mayonnaise. Perfect for a grilled cheese, PB&J, chicken club sandwich, pimento cheese sandwich, diner burger, pizza toast, or a butter-and-ham sandwich!

THIS RECIPE MAKES 1 PAN LOAF OF ABOUT 1¾ POUNDS.

First rise
3 to 3½ hours at 70°F / 21°C room temperature.
Faster if warmer, slower if cooler.

Proof time
About 1 hour at 70°F / 21°C room temperature.

Bake
Preheat to 450°F / 230°C for 45 minutes,
bake at 425°F / 220°C for about 50 minutes.

Sample schedule
Begin at 9:30 a.m., finish mixing at 10 a.m.,
shape into a loaf at 1:30 p.m., and bake at 2:30 p.m.

Ingredient	Quantity	Baker's Percentage
White bread flour	500 g / 3½ cups + 1 Tbsp + 1 tsp	100%
Water (90° to 95°F / 32° to 35°C)	370 g / 1½ cups + 2 tsp	74%
Fine sea salt	11 g / 2¼ tsp	2.2%
Instant dried yeast	3 g / 1 tsp	0.6%
Levain (optional)	100 g / ½ cup	9% of total flour (if used)

1. Autolyse

Measure 370 grams (90° to 95°F / 32° to 35°C) water into a 6-quart round tub or similar container. If you have a levain, add 100 grams from the refrigerator—you can weigh it directly into the dough tub with its water. Stir a bit with your fingers to loosen up the culture. Add 500 grams white bread flour. Mix it by hand until all is incorporated.

Sprinkle 11 grams fine sea salt evenly across the top of the autolyse dough. Then sprinkle 3 grams instant dried yeast on top of that. Let them rest there, where they will partially dissolve.

Cover and let rest for 15 to 20 minutes.

2. Mix

Mix by hand, wetting your working hand before mixing so the dough doesn't stick to you. Reach underneath the dough and grab about one-fourth of it. Gently stretch this section and fold it over the top to the other side of the dough. Repeat three more times with the remaining dough until the salt and yeast are fully enclosed.

Use the pincer method to fully integrate the ingredients. Make five or six pincer cuts across the entire mass of dough. Then fold the dough over itself a few times. Repeat, alternately cutting and folding, until all the ingredients are fully integrated. Let the dough rest for a few minutes, then fold for another 30 seconds or until the dough tightens up. The whole process should take about 5 minutes. The target dough temperature at the end of the mix is about 75°F / 24°C. Cover the tub and let the dough rise until the next fold.

3. Fold & First Rise

This dough needs two folds (see page 41). It's easiest to apply the folds during the first hour after mixing the dough. Apply the first fold about 10 minutes after mixing and the second when you see the dough spread out in the tub. If need be, it's okay to fold later; just be sure to leave it alone for the last hour of rising.

When the dough is two and a half to three times its original volume, 3 to 3½ hours after the mix, it's ready to be made up into a loaf and put into its pan. If you are using a 6-quart dough tub, the ideal point is when the edge of the dough has reached just shy (about ¼ inch) of the 2-quart line on the side of the tub, and the dough will be domed—not flattened, not collapsed. If it reaches the 2-quart line on your dough tub, that's fine too. It'll be best if you don't let it go beyond that, as you want to preserve what's left of the rise for the next stage, in the pan. If the room is cool and the dough is taking longer, let it continue to rise until it reaches this amount of volume expansion. If you're not using a marked dough tub, you'll have to eyeball it. Use your best judgment.

4. Remove the Dough from Its Tub

Lightly flour a work surface about 12 inches wide. Flour your hands and sprinkle a bit of flour around the edges of the tub. Tip the tub slightly and gently work your floured free hand beneath the dough to loosen it from the bottom of the tub. Then turn the tub on its side and ease the dough onto the work surface without pulling or tearing it.

Even if your bread pan is nonstick, you might want to give it a light spritz of cooking spray. Nonstick pans are sometimes not 100 percent nonstick if they have been used a lot.

5. Shape

With floured hands, pick up the dough and ease it back onto the work surface in a somewhat even, rectangular shape. You will stretch and fold this slack dough into something equal to the width of your bread pan.

Following the shaping instructions on pages 43 to 44, with two floured hands, stretch the dough, simultaneously pulling it right and left (just spread your hands both ways at the same time to stretch out the dough) until it resists—two to three times its original width—and then fold the ends back over each other, creating a "packet" the width of your baking pan.

Brush off any loose flour from the top of the dough and do a roll-up motion from the bottom up or from top to bottom to form a tube of dough that's about the same width as your baking pan. Place the dough seam-up into the pan. The seam is usually visible; it's the part of the rolled-up dough where the outer edges have joined to enclose the interior parts of the newly shaped loaf.

Don't stress this. It takes repeated efforts to learn the hand skills to shape sticky, slack bread dough. The pan does much of the work for you, so if all you can manage is to get the dough into the pan, you are not a failure. It'll work fine. Dough bits will stick to your fingers; with time, you will get used to it. My trick is to always grab the dough by its driest outside and flour-covered bottom parts that aren't so sticky. Just avoid leaving any loose flour inside the dough before you roll it up into the pan shape.

6. Proof

Use your hand to apply a light film of water across the entire top surface of the dough after it's in its pan. Then place your bread pan in a nonperforated plastic bag, but do not make it tight at the top. Leave plenty of room for the dough to expand, a few inches, and tuck the bag under the pan. It doesn't need to be airtight. The point of the bag is to keep the dough from drying out during the next hour of proof time.

With my usual bread pan (8½ by 4½ by 2¾ inches), I like to see the dough rising a bit above the rim of the pan before baking, but you can't let it go too far above or it will collapse over the edge. If your pan is larger, the dough likely won't rise above its rim. See photos of perfect proofing on page 50.

Plan on baking the loaf about an hour after it is shaped, assuming a room temperature of about 70°F / 21°C. If your kitchen is warmer, it will be optimally proofed earlier.

7. Preheat

About 45 minutes prior to baking, position a rack in the middle of the oven and preheat the oven to 450°F / 230°C.

8. Bake

Remove the pan from the plastic bag and place it on the center of the oven rack. Turn down the heat to 425°F / 220°C and bake. After 30 minutes, check for even baking (give the pan a turn if the baking is uneven) and bake for another 20 minutes. (If you are baking in a lidded pan, keep the lid in place throughout, but you can check on it near the end to judge how much time to finish.) Because this dough has more water than traditional pan loaves, it needs a longer time than you might think to bake the inside fully and to color the sides and give them enough strength to avoid post-bake collapse.

After 50 minutes, the top of the loaf should be darkly colored (use the photo on page 57 as a reference). The sides and bottom should not be as dark as the top. (A lidded-pan loaf will bake to a lighter color; while I recommend 50 minutes baking time, open the lid and check at 45 minutes for color in case your oven runs a little hot.)

Remove the pan with oven mitts or thick kitchen towels and carefully tilt it to turn the loaf out. If a hard rap on the counter doesn't free the loaf, use a folded kitchen towel to firmly grab one edge of the pan with one hand and use your other hand to pry the loaf out. (Use more cooking spray next time.) Let the loaf cool on a rack, so air can circulate around it, at least 30 minutes before slicing; 1 hour is better.

50% EMMER OR EINKORN BREAD

Open pan, lidded pan, or Dutch oven

The flavor of breads baked with emmer or einkorn is rich and nutty—more flavorful, really—than those made from standard wheat flours. Emmer and einkorn are genetically simpler than standard, modern wheat varieties and also have a lower quantity of gluten, which some people claim leads to improved digestibility for these breads.

Emmer and einkorn are distinct wheat grains with different histories, yet they work equally well with this formula, and both are now likely to be available in the United States from roughly the same groups of farmers and mills that are part of the "artisan wheat" or "craft mill" movement. I get similar results with these two grains. I buy both flours from Camas Country Mill in Eugene, Oregon. Bluebird Grain Farms, Barton Springs Mill, Janie's Mill, Bench View Farms, Grist & Toll, and others around the United States have these available online. See what you can find that's near you. You can also substitute heritage whole-wheat varieties such as Turkey Red, Amorojo, or others offered by your favorite mill.

The germ of the grain gets crushed in the stone milling, and it's like a flavorful fat has been added to the dough (the germ contains healthful fats, and it is the most nutritious part of the wheat kernel). One happy result is that, when toasted, this bread has an extra bit of crispness. Think of the way that a milk bread or brioche crisps when toasted—this, too, has that wonderfully light-textured crunch.

Despite this bread's weaker-than-usual gluten, I get a very good rise when I blend emmer or einkorn with an equal amount of bread flour; which helps this loaf get a rise at least equivalent to The Standard loaf on page 81: almost 5 inches from bottom to top in my USA Pan.

THIS RECIPE MAKES 1 PAN LOAF OF A LITTLE MORE THAN 2 POUNDS.

First rise
3 to 3½ hours at 70°F / 21°C room temperature.
Faster if warmer, slower if cooler.

Proof time
About 1 hour at 70°F / 21°C room temperature.

Bake
Preheat to 450°F / 230°C for 45 minutes,
bake at 425°F / 220°C for about 50 minutes.

Sample schedule
Begin at 9:30 a.m., finish mixing at 10 a.m.,
shape into a loaf at 1:30 p.m., and bake at 2:30 p.m.

Ingredient	Quantity	Baker's Percentage
Whole-grain emmer or einkorn flour	250 g / 1¾ cups + 1¾ tsp	50%
White bread flour	250 g / 1¾ cups + 1¾ tsp	50%
Water (90° to 95°F / 32° to 35°C)	425 g / 1¾ cups + 1 tsp	85%
Fine sea salt	11 g / 2¼ tsp	2.2%
Instant dried yeast	3 g / 1 tsp	0.6%
Levain (optional)	100 g / ½ cup	9% of total flour (if used)

1. Autolyse

Measure 425 grams (90° to 95°F / 32° to 35°C) water into a 6-quart round tub or similar container. If you have a levain, add 100 grams from the refrigerator—you can weigh it directly into the dough tub with its water. Stir a bit with your fingers to loosen up the culture. Add 250 grams emmer or einkorn flour and 250 grams white bread flour. Mix it by hand until all is incorporated.

Sprinkle 11 grams fine sea salt evenly across the top of the autolyse dough. Then sprinkle 3 grams instant dried yeast on top of that. Let them rest there, where they will partially dissolve.

Cover and let rest for 30 minutes.

2. Mix

Mix by hand, wetting your working hand before mixing so the dough doesn't stick to you. Reach underneath the dough and grab about one-fourth of it. Gently stretch this section and fold it over the top to the other side of the dough. Repeat three more times with the remaining dough until the salt and yeast are fully enclosed.

Use the pincer method to fully integrate the ingredients. Make five or six pincer cuts across the entire mass of dough. Then fold the dough over itself a few times. Repeat, alternately cutting and folding, until all the ingredients are fully integrated. Let the dough rest for a few minutes, then fold for another 30 seconds or until the dough tightens up. The whole process should take about 5 minutes. The target dough temperature at the end of the mix is about 75°F / 24°C. Cover the tub and let the dough rise until the next fold.

3. Fold & First Rise

This dough needs two folds (see page 41). It's easiest to apply the folds during the first hour after mixing the dough. Apply the first fold about 10 minutes after mixing and the second when you see the dough spread out in the tub. If need be, it's okay to fold later; just be sure to leave it alone for the last hour of rising.

When the dough is two and a half to three times its original volume, 3 to 3½ hours after the mix, it's ready to be made up into a loaf and put into its pan. If you are using a 6-quart dough tub, the ideal point is when the edge of the dough has reached just shy (about ¼ inch) of the 2-quart line on the side of the tub, and the dough will be domed—not flattened, not collapsed. If it reaches the 2-quart line on your dough tub, that's fine too. It'll be best if you don't let it go beyond that, as you want to preserve what's left of the rise for the next stage, in the pan. If the room is cool and the dough is taking longer, let it continue to rise until it reaches this amount of volume expansion. If you're not using a marked dough tub, you'll have to eyeball it. Use your best judgment.

4. Remove the Dough from Its Tub

Moderately flour a work surface about 12 inches wide. Flour your hands and sprinkle a bit of flour around the edges of the tub. Tip the tub slightly and gently work your floured free hand beneath the dough to loosen it from the bottom of the tub. Then turn the tub on its side and ease the dough onto the work surface without pulling or tearing it.

Even if your bread pan is nonstick, you might want to give it a light spritz of cooking spray. Nonstick pans are sometimes not 100 percent nonstick if they have been used a lot.

5. Shape

With floured hands, pick up the dough and ease it back onto the work surface in a somewhat even, rectangular shape. You will stretch and fold this slack dough into something equal to the width of your bread pan.

Following the shaping instructions on pages 43 to 44, with two floured hands, stretch the dough, simultaneously pulling it right and left (just spread your hands both ways at the same time to stretch out the dough) until it resists—two to three times its original width—and then fold the ends back over each other, creating a "packet" the width of your baking pan.

Brush off any loose flour from the top of the dough and do a roll-up motion from the bottom up or from top to bottom to form a tube of dough that's about the same width as your baking pan. Place the dough seam-up into the pan. The seam is usually visible; it's the part of the rolled-up dough where the outer edges have joined to enclose the interior parts of the newly shaped loaf.

Don't stress this. It takes repeated efforts to learn the hand skills to shape sticky, slack bread dough. The pan does much of the work for you, so if all you can manage is to get the dough into the pan, you are not a failure. It'll work fine. Dough bits will stick to your fingers; with time, you will get used to it. My trick is always to grab the dough by its driest outside and flour-covered bottom parts that aren't so sticky. Just avoid leaving any loose flour inside the dough before you roll it up into the pan shape.

6. Proof

Use your hand to apply a light film of water across the entire top surface of the dough after it's in its pan. Then place your bread pan in a nonperforated plastic bag, but do not make it tight at the top. Leave plenty of room for the dough to expand, a few inches, and tuck the bag under the pan. It doesn't need to be airtight. The point of the bag is to keep the dough from drying out during the next hour of proof time.

With my usual bread pan (8½ by 4½ by 2¾ inches), I like to see the dough rising a bit above the rim of the pan before baking, but you can't let it go too far above or it will collapse over the edge. If your pan is larger, the dough likely won't rise above its rim. See photos of perfect proofing on page 50.

Plan on baking the loaf about an hour after it is shaped, assuming a room temperature of about 70°F / 21°C. If your kitchen is warmer, it will be optimally proofed earlier.

7. Preheat

About 45 minutes prior to baking, position a rack in the middle of the oven and preheat the oven to 450°F / 230°C.

8. Bake

Remove the pan from the plastic bag and place it on the center of the oven rack. Turn down the heat to 425°F / 220°C and bake. After 30 minutes, check for even baking (give the pan a turn if the baking is uneven) and bake for another 20 minutes. Because this dough has more water than traditional pan loaves, it needs a longer time than you might think to bake the inside fully and to color the sides and give them enough strength to avoid post-bake collapse.

After 50 minutes, the top of the loaf should be darkly colored. The sides and bottom should not be as dark as the top.

Remove the pan with oven mitts or thick kitchen towels and carefully tilt it to turn the loaf out. If a hard rap on the counter doesn't free the loaf, use a folded kitchen towel to firmly grab one edge of the pan with one hand and use the other hand to pry the loaf out. (Use more cooking spray next time.) Let the loaf cool on a rack, so air can circulate around it, for at least 30 minutes before slicing; 1 hour is better.

What Exactly are Ancient Wheat Grains?

Einkorn, emmer, and spelt grew wild in the ancient world and became among the earliest farmed crops. Einkorn was likely the first wheat that humans cultivated, perhaps beginning around ten thousand years ago. Contemporary scientists have mapped the genetic histories of all these early wheat varieties, and archaeological findings have traced their use to the foods and beverages of ancient societies and nomads. Among these discoveries is Ötzi the Iceman, found frozen in the Italian Alps in 1991 (he lived about five thousand years ago), who revealed evidence of einkorn in his diet. All three of these ancient wheat varieties are favorites of mine for their flavor. The yield in farmers' fields is lower than what is possible with modern-day wheat varieties, so these grains are a little more expensive.

50% RYE BREAD

Open pan, lidded pan, or Dutch oven

In France, a half-rye-flour, half-wheat-flour bread cannot be called *pain de seigle* (rye bread), because it needs to have at least 63 percent rye flour to be labeled "seigle," or rye. Truth in labeling! In the United States, we have a much different idea of what rye bread is—a lighter style with no rules about how much rye is in the dough (we regulate rye whiskey but not rye bread). The usual American rye bread actually contains more wheat flour than rye flour to make it lightly textured, as with the New York–style rye bread recipe on page 159.

A friend asked me why rye breads taste like caraway. It seems like a funny question, but to so many people, rye and caraway are linked in flavor in all their rye bread experiences, maybe due to deli sandwiches. This recipe, however, is closer to a true rye bread, a hearty and somewhat dense, flavorful loaf; albeit really plain looking, so its charm is sneaky. It's a good, easy intro to real rye bread. If you like it, you should graduate to the more involved sourdough version on page 221 (the suggested addition of walnuts is very highly recommended).

Rye flour has much weaker gluten than wheat flour does, and loaves made with a significant percentage of rye, like this recipe, benefit from a preshape, a rest of about 10 minutes, and then a final shape before putting it into its pan. This will build up the gluten strength and allow for the best possible rise. They also bake smaller and denser than wheat breads.

I like how the baking pan supports the weaker gluten of rye, giving structure for this loaf's rise. You will get a respectable volume and texture in the finished bread. It should measure about 4¼ inches in height (compared with The Standard loaf at 5 inches). Slicing it thinly is my preference since the rye is dense and chewy.

THIS RECIPE MAKES 1 PAN LOAF OF ABOUT 2 POUNDS.

First rise
About 3½ hours at 70°F / 21°C room temperature.
Faster if warmer, slower if cooler.

Proof time
About 45 minutes at 70°F / 21°C room temperature.

Bake
Preheat to 450°F / 230°C for 45 minutes,
bake at 425°F / 220°C for about 50 minutes.

Sample schedule
Begin at 9:30 a.m., finish mixing at 10 a.m.,
shape into a loaf at 1:30 p.m., and bake at 2:15 p.m.

Ingredient	Quantity	Baker's Percentage
White bread flour	250 g / 1¾ cups + 1¾ tsp	50%
Whole or dark rye flour	250 g / 1¾ cups + 2 Tbsp + 2¼ tsp	50%
Water (90° to 95°F / 32° to 35°C)	390 g / 1½ cups + 2 Tbsp	78%
Fine sea salt	11 g / 2¼ tsp	2.2%
Instant dried yeast	3 g / 1 tsp	0.6%
Levain (optional)	100 g / ½ cup	9% of total flour (if used)

1. Autolyse

Measure 390 grams (90° to 95°F / 32° to 35°C) water into a 6-quart round tub or similar container. If you have a levain, add 100 grams from the refrigerator—you can weigh it directly into the dough tub with its water. Stir a bit with your fingers to loosen up the culture. Add 250 grams white bread flour and 250 grams whole or dark rye flour. Mix it by hand until all is incorporated.

Sprinkle 11 grams fine sea salt evenly across the top of the dough. Then sprinkle 3 grams instant dry yeast on top of that. Let them rest there, where they will partially dissolve.

Cover and let rest for 20 to 30 minutes.

2. Mix

Mix by hand, wetting your working hand before mixing so the dough doesn't stick to you. (Rye dough is especially sticky, so you just need to get used to it, but a wet hand is essential.) Reach underneath the dough and grab about one-fourth of it. Gently stretch this section and fold it over the top to the other side of the dough. Repeat three more times with the remaining dough until the salt and yeast are fully enclosed. (You'll notice the rye dough doesn't stretch as much as the doughs made with just wheat flour.)

Use the pincer method to fully integrate the ingredients. Make five or six pincer cuts across the entire mass of dough. Then fold the dough over itself a few times. Repeat, alternately cutting and folding, until all the ingredients are fully integrated. Let the dough rest for a few minutes, then fold for another 30 seconds or until the dough tightens up. The whole process should take about 5 minutes. The target dough temperature

at the end of the mix is about 75°F / 24°C. Cover the tub and let the dough rise until the next fold.

3. Fold & First Rise

This dough needs two folds (see page 41). Apply the folds during the first hour after mixing the dough. Apply the first fold about 10 minutes after mixing and the second when you see the dough spread out in the tub. If need be, it's okay to fold later; just be sure to leave it alone for the last hour of rising.

When the dough is about two and a half times its original volume, 3 to 3½ hours after the mix, it's ready to be made up into a loaf and put into its pan. If you are using a 6-quart dough tub, the ideal point is when the edge of the dough has reached just shy (about ¼ inch) of the 2-quart line on the side of the tub, and the dough will be domed—not flattened, not collapsed. Do not let it go beyond that. If the room is cool and the dough is taking longer, let it continue to rise it reaches this amount of volume expansion. If you're not using a marked dough tub, you'll have to eyeball it. Use your best judgment.

4. Remove the Dough from Its Tub

Moderately flour a work surface about 12 inches wide. Flour your hands and sprinkle a bit of flour around the edges of the tub. Tip the tub slightly and gently work your floured free hand beneath the dough to loosen it from the bottom of the tub. Then turn the tub on its side and ease the dough out onto the work surface without pulling or tearing it.

Even if your bread pan is nonstick, you might want to give it a light spritz of cooking spray.

5a. Preshape

With floured hands, pick up the dough and ease it back onto the work surface in a somewhat even, rectangular shape.

Holding part of the dough with one hand, use your other hand to stretch the dough out until it resists, then fold it back over itself. Give it a quarter turn and repeat over and over until you have formed a medium-tight round of dough. The motion is stretch-and-fold a few times until the ball of dough resists. Cover and let rest for about 15 minutes.

5b. Shape

Stretch and fold the dough and use whatever motion works for you to form it into a rectangular shape about the width of your bread pan. Do a roll-up motion from the bottom up or from top to bottom to form a tube of dough that's about the same width as your baking pan. Place the dough seam-up into the pan. The seam is usually visible; it's the part of the rolled-up dough where the outer edges have joined to enclose the interior parts of the newly shaped loaf.

Don't stress this; just get it into the pan. It takes repeated efforts to learn the hand skills to shape sticky rye dough, but this dough is tolerant, and you should get good results each time you make this.

6. Proof

You can give this dough a light film of water on top to prevent sticking as the dough rises, but it's not usually needed; it won't rise as much as the lighter bread doughs will. Place your bread pan in a nonperforated plastic bag, and tuck the bag under the pan. It doesn't need to be airtight. The point of the bag is to keep the dough from drying out during the next 45 minutes of proof time.

Plan on baking the loaf about 45 minutes after it is shaped, assuming a room temperature of about 70°F / 21°C. If your kitchen is warmer, it will be optimally proofed earlier.

7. Preheat

About 45 minutes prior to baking, position a rack in the middle of the oven and preheat the oven to 450°F / 230°C.

8. Bake

Remove the pan from the plastic bag and place it on the center of the oven rack. Turn down the heat to 425°F / 220°C and bake. After 30 minutes, check for even baking (give the pan a turn if the baking is uneven) and bake for another 20 minutes.

After 50 minutes, the top of the loaf should be darkly colored. The sides and bottom should not be as dark as the top.

Remove the pan with oven mitts or thick kitchen towels and carefully tilt it to turn the loaf out. If a hard rap on the counter doesn't free the loaf, use a folded kitchen towel to firmly grab one edge of the pan with one hand and use the other hand to pry the loaf out. (Use more cooking spray next time.) Let the loaf cool on a rack, so air can circulate around it, for at least 30 minutes before slicing; 1 hour is better.

Above: 50% Rye Bread (left), New York–Style Rye Bread with Caraway (right)

Below: Three breads with rye flour. Raisin-Pecan Bread (right)

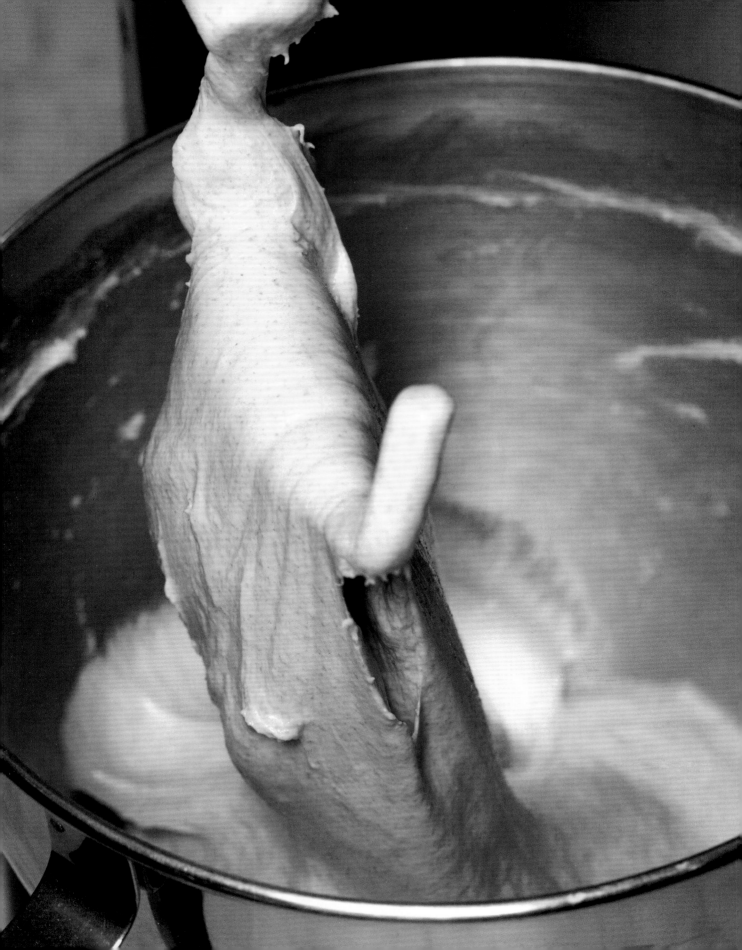

BUTTER BREAD

Open pan, lidded pan, or Dutch oven

This recipe requires a stand mixer with a 4- to 5-quart mixing bowl and a dough hook

Make a bread dough and then mix in cubes of cold, delicious butter. It's got to work, right? That's what I told myself as I was imagining this too-obvious idea that had somehow eluded me for the last twenty-some years.

I have a KitchenAid Professional model that frowns at me every time I mix bread dough by hand; now it's showtime. Still, I mix this dough first by hand as with all my other unenriched bread doughs. Then the dough goes into a 4½-quart mixer bowl (other sizes should work), and I add cubes of just-from-the-fridge butter that have been lightly coated with flour. The flour gives the butter some grip, and it aids integration into the dough. Mix for a few minutes on low speed and then about 5 minutes on the mixer's medium-high speed until none of the butter pieces are visible.

This process is a standard bakery technique for mixing butter into dough. Brioche and pain de mie are two classic examples. They have milk, eggs, sugar, and butter in varying proportions, while this is just flour, water, salt, yeast, and butter. The butter provides more food for the yeast, and, along with the intense mix, the dough has a very active fermentation. The last hour of the first rise is in the refrigerator (make sure you have room) both to slow down the dough and to ease shaping into a loaf after it's done.

At some point while it is baking, you'll be enveloped by a smell that reminds you that life can be wonderful. The aroma of any bread baking is great, but this one is cartoonishly fantastic. It is so worth the effort, and I especially like it lightly toasted. It gets a beautiful thinly crisped, buttery, delicate crunch. The fragrant wake of it toasting is hot, humid, and passionate. Perfect with jam, ham, and as a sandwich bread.

Butter Bread works well in a lidded pan. Let the dough rise to within ¼ inch of the lid, or even touching the lid, before putting into at 425°F / 220°C oven. Bake for about 45 minutes.

THIS RECIPE MAKES 1 PAN LOAF OF ABOUT 2 POUNDS.

First rise
About 2 hours at 70°F / 21°C room temperature,
and 1 hour more in the refrigerator.

Proof time
About 1¼ hours at 70°F / 21°C room temperature.

Bake
Preheat to 450°F / 230°C for 45 minutes,
bake at 425°F / 220°C for about 50 minutes.

Sample schedule
Begin at 9:30 a.m., finish mixing at 10 a.m., transfer to the refrigerator
at noon, shape into a loaf at 1 p.m., and bake at 2:15 p.m.

Ingredient	Quantity	Baker's Percentage
White bread flour*	400 g / 2¾ cups + 2 tsp	80%
Whole-wheat flour	100 g / ½ cup + 3 Tbsp + 1¼ tsp	20%
Water (90° to 95°F / 32° to 35°C)*	370 g / 1½ cups + 2 tsp	74%
Fine sea salt	11 g / 2¼ tsp	2.2%
Instant dried yeast	3 g / 1 tsp	0.6%
Levain (optional)	100 g / ½ cup	9% of total flour (if used)
Butter, cubed (cold)	100 g / ¼ cup + 3 Tbsp + ¾ tsp	20%

* If you want to use all white bread flour, increase the amount to 500 grams / 3½ cups + 1 Tbsp + ½ tsp and decrease the water to 360 grams / 1½ cups.

1a. Autolyse

Measure 370 grams (90° to 95°F / 32° to 35°C) water into a 6-quart round tub or similar container. If you have a levain, add 100 grams from the refrigerator—you can weigh it directly into the dough tub with its water. Stir a bit with your fingers to loosen up the culture. Add 400 grams white bread flour and 100 grams whole-wheat flour. Mix it by hand until all is incorporated.

Sprinkle 11 grams fine sea salt evenly across the top of the autolyse dough. Then sprinkle 3 grams instant dried yeast on top of that. Let them rest there, where they will partially dissolve.

Cover and let rest for 15 to 20 minutes.

1b. Cube the Butter

Weigh 100 grams cold butter (straight from the fridge) on your scale. (Put an empty container, paper towel, or piece of parchment on the scale, hit "tare" or "zero," and then weigh the butter in the container or on the paper towel or parchment.)

Use a baker's bench knife or just a regular kitchen knife to cut the butter into about a dozen chunks the size of grapes. Toss the butter chunks with about 20 grams / 2 Tbsp + 1 tsp white bread flour and then discard the excess flour. Let it sit out while you mix the dough.

2a. Mix

Mix the dough by hand, wetting your working hand before mixing so the dough doesn't stick to you. Reach underneath the dough and grab about one-fourth of it. Gently stretch this section and fold it over the top to the other side of the dough. Repeat three more times with the remaining dough until the salt and yeast are fully enclosed.

Use the pincer method to fully integrate the ingredients. Make five or six pincer cuts across the entire mass of dough. Then fold the dough over itself a few times. Repeat, alternately cutting and folding, until all the ingredients are fully integrated. Let the dough rest for a few minutes, then fold for another 30 seconds or until the dough tightens up. The whole process should take about 5 minutes. The target dough temperature at the end of the mix is 75°F / 24°C.

2b. Butter Up!

Finish the mix in a stand mixer fitted with a dough hook attachment. Wet your hand and punch down the dough with a fist, then put it into the mixer. Put the butter pieces on top. Mix on low speed for about 2 minutes to begin and then on the medium-high setting for about 5 minutes, or until all the butter is incorporated into the dough. You don't want a violent high speed. It should be just fast enough to emulsify the butter into the dough. My KitchenAid has 6 speed settings, and I use number 4 for this stage. Run it until you see no more butter chunks. If, when you remove the dough, you spot a few small butter chunks you didn't notice before, no worries. It'll be fine. The final dough temperature should remain about what it was before: 75°F / 24°C. The heat generated by friction from the high-speed mixing and the cold butter cancel each other out.

Pull the dough out of the mixer, fold it up on a lightly floured work surface to give it a little tension, and return it to your dough tub to rise.

3. Fold & First Rise

This dough needs just one fold (see page 41).
Do this fold during the first hour after mixing in
the butter and transferring it to the dough tub.

About 2 hours after the end of the butter mix, the
dough should be two and a half to three times its
original volume. It's faster than the other bread
doughs. Transfer the dough, in its tub, to the refrigerator for 1 hour. If you are using a 6-quart dough
tub, the ideal point at the end of the rise is when the
edge of the dough has reached all the way up to the
2-quart line on the side of the tub, and the dough
will be domed—not flattened, not collapsed. It'll be
best if you don't let it go beyond that, as you want
to preserve what's left of the rise for the next stage,
in the pan. If you're not using a marked dough tub,
you'll have to eyeball it. Use your best judgment.

4. Remove the Dough from Its Tub

Lightly flour a work surface about 12 inches wide.
Flour your hands and sprinkle a bit of flour around
the edges of the tub. Tip the tub slightly and gently
work your floured free hand beneath the dough to
loosen it from the bottom of the tub. Then turn the
tub on its side and ease the dough out onto the work
surface without pulling or tearing it.

Even if your bread pan is nonstick, you might want
to give it a light spritz of cooking spray. Nonstick
pans are sometimes not 100 percent nonstick if they
have been used a lot.

5. Shape

With floured hands, pick up the dough and ease it back
onto the work surface in a somewhat even, rectangular shape. You will stretch and fold this slack dough
into something equal to the width of your bread pan.

Following the shaping instructions on pages 43 to
44, with two floured hands, stretch the dough,
simultaneously pulling it right and left (just spread
your hands both ways at the same time to stretch out
the dough) until it resists—three times its original
width—and then fold the ends back over each other,
creating a "packet" the width of your baking pan.
This buttered dough will feel a little slicker and will
stretch a bit farther than other doughs.

Brush off any loose flour from the top of the dough and
do a roll-up motion from the bottom up or from top to
bottom to form a tube of dough that's about the same
width as your baking pan. Place the dough seam-up
into the pan. The seam is usually visible; it's the part of
the rolled-up dough where the outer edges have joined
to enclose the interior parts of the newly shaped loaf.

6. Proof

Use your hand to apply a light film of water across
the entire top surface of the dough after it's in its
pan. Then place your bread pan in a nonperforated
plastic bag, but do not make it tight at the top. Leave
plenty of room for the dough to expand, a few inches,
and tuck the bag under the pan. It doesn't need to
be airtight. The point of the bag is to keep the dough
from drying out during the next hour of proof time.

With my usual bread pan (8½ by 4½ by 2¾ inches),
I like to see the dough rising a bit above the rim of
the pan before baking, but you can't let it go too far

above or it will collapse over the edge. If your pan is larger, the dough likely won't rise above its rim. See photos of perfect proofing on page 50.

Plan on baking the loaf about an hour after it is shaped, assuming a room temperature of about 70°F / 21°C. If your kitchen is warmer, it will be optimally proofed earlier.

7. Preheat

About 45 minutes prior to baking, position a rack in the middle of the oven and preheat the oven to 450°F / 230°C.

8. Bake

Remove the pan from the plastic bag and place it on the center of the oven rack. Turn down the heat to 425°F / 220°C and bake. After 30 minutes, check for even baking (give the pan a turn if the baking is uneven) and bake for another 20 minutes. Because this dough has more water than traditional pan loaves, it needs a longer time than you might think to bake the inside fully and to color the sides and give them enough strength to avoid post-bake collapse.

After 50 minutes, the top of the loaf should be a beautiful golden brown.

Remove the pan with oven mitts or thick kitchen towels and carefully tilt it to turn the loaf out. If a hard rap on the counter doesn't free the loaf, use a folded kitchen towel to firmly grab one edge of the pan with one hand and use your other hand to pry the loaf out. (Use more cooking spray next time.) Let the loaf cool on a rack, so air can circulate around it, for about 30 minutes before slicing.

BLACK BREAD

Lidded pan, open pan, or Dutch oven

This dramatic loaf can turn out more purple than black. The purple comes from this recipe's addition of black rice flour. The rest of the dark color is from dark beer and whole or dark rye flour. I like using Guinness stout to hydrate the dough. You could also use a porter, a different stout, or a dark ale.

I'll eat this bread with fresh cheeses, sausages, pickled vegetables, cured fish, or egg salad. It's excellent as a base for canapés. It's also a good platform for a spread of soft goat cheese and sliced hard-boiled egg with mayonnaise, or for mini sandwiches with butter and ham. I like to put small croutons made from this bread on salads.

Breads such as this that are very dark, even if they aren't fully black, have long been referred to as "black breads," such as Germany's Schwarzbrot, and are almost always made with rye flour. Pumpernickel is a good example. A true pumpernickel gets its dark color from the very long baking in a low-temperature oven in a lidded pan; to the point that a Maillard reaction occurs not just in the crust, where we are used to seeing that browning happen, but in the inside of the loaf as well. The lidded pan keeps the moisture in while all of this is going on, and the 100 percent rye versions of these breads are very dense and dark. However, most black breads these days get their dark color from additives, such as dark molasses, cocoa powder, coffee (or instant coffee flakes), and even charcoal (don't go there!), rather than a very long bake.

I like this recipe best when baked in the lidded bread pan, which is what I give instructions for here. The loaf will bake into an even form with squared-off edges. For my equipment selections, see page 28. If you don't have a lidded pan, try this recipe as a pan bread in any open pan you have used for the other recipes in this book.

This dough includes a modest amount of brown sugar, but the final bread is not sweet at all. The brown sugar offsets the natural, slightly bitter flavors of the black rice flour and the stout beer.

You may have to order the black rice flour online, as I did.

THIS RECIPE MAKES 1 PAN LOAF OF ABOUT 2¾ POUNDS.

First rise
About 3½ hours at 70°F / 21°C room temperature. Faster if warmer, slower if cooler.

Proof time
About 1¼ hours at 70°F / 21°C room temperature.

Bake
Preheat to 450°F / 230°C for 45 minutes, bake at 425°F / 220°C for 30 minutes, then at 375°F / 190°C for another 30 minutes.

Sample schedule
Begin at 12:30 p.m., finish mixing at 1 p.m., shape into a loaf at 4:30 p.m., and bake at 5:45 p.m. Let cool overnight or for a minimum of 1 hour.

Ingredient	Quantity	Baker's Percentage
White bread flour*	250 g / 1¾ cups + 1¾ tsp	50%
Whole or dark rye flour*	150 g / 1 cup + 2 Tbsp + 1½ tsp	30%
Whole-wheat flour*	100 g / ½ cup + 3 Tbsp + 1¼ tsp	20%
Black rice flour*	100 g / ⅔ cup	20%
Guinness stout (90° to 95°F / 32° to 35°C)	250 g / 1 cup + 2 tsp	50%
Water (90° to 95°F / 32° to 35°C)	250 g / 1 cup + 2 tsp	50%
Brown sugar	15 g / 1 Tbsp + ½ tsp	3%
Fine sea salt	13 g / 2½ tsp	2.6%
Instant dried yeast	3 g / 1 tsp	0.6%
Levain (optional)	100 g / ½ cup	9% of total flour (if used)

* *I only include flour that leavens in the 100% marker. These baker's percentages consider the black rice flour as an additive ingredient. The 100 percent flour total is the white bread flour plus rye flour plus whole-wheat flour only. All other baker's percentages are calculated against these three flours.*

1. Autolyse

Measure 250 grams white bread flour, 150 grams rye flour, 100 grams whole-wheat flour, and 100 grams black rice flour into a container, then blend them by hand. In a small saucepan, warm 250 grams Guinness stout until it reaches 90° to 95°F / 32° to 35°C—it happens fast, so don't walk away—then put it into a 6-quart round tub or similar container and add 250 grams (90° to 95°F / 32° to 35°C) water. If you have a levain, add 100 grams from the refrigerator—you can weigh it directly into the dough tub with its liquid. Stir a bit with your fingers to loosen up the culture. Add the blended flours. Mix by hand just until incorporated. This will make a sticky but cohesive dough.

Sprinkle 13 grams fine sea salt and 15 grams brown sugar evenly across the top of the autolyse dough. Then sprinkle 3 grams of instant dried yeast on top of that. Let them rest there, where they will partially dissolve.

Cover and let rest 15 to 20 minutes.

2. Mix

Mix by hand, wetting your working hand before mixing so the dough doesn't stick to you. Reach underneath the dough and grab about one-fourth of it. Gently stretch this section and fold it over the top to the other side of the dough. Repeat three more times with the remaining dough until the salt and yeast are fully enclosed. (You'll notice the rye dough doesn't stretch as much as the doughs made with just wheat flour.)

Use the pincer method to fully integrate the ingredients. Make five or six pincer cuts across the entire mass of dough. Then fold the dough over itself a few times. Repeat, alternately cutting and folding, until all the ingredients are fully integrated. Let the dough rest for a few minutes, then fold for another 30 seconds or until the dough tightens up. The whole process should take about 5 minutes. The target dough temperature at the end of the mix is 77° to 78°F / 25° to 26°C. Cover the tub and let the dough rise until the next fold.

3. Fold & First Rise

This dough needs two folds (see page 41). It's easiest to apply the folds during the first hour after mixing the dough. Apply the first fold about 10 minutes after mixing and the second when you see the dough spread out in the tub. If need be, it's okay to fold later; just be sure to leave it alone for the last hour of rising.

When the dough is two and a half times its original volume, about 3½ hours after the mix, it's ready to be made up into a loaf and put into its pan. If you are using a 6-quart dough tub, the ideal point is when the edge of the dough has reached all the way up to the 2-quart line on the side of the tub, and dough will be domed—not flattened, not collapsed. If you're not using a marked dough tub, you'll have to eyeball it. Use your best judgment.

4. Remove the Dough from Its Tub

Moderately flour a work surface about 12 inches wide. Flour your hands and sprinkle a bit of flour around the edges of the tub. Tip the tub slightly and gently work your floured free hand beneath the dough to loosen it from the bottom of the tub. Then turn the tub on its side and ease the dough out onto the work surface without pulling or tearing it.

Even if your bread pan is nonstick, you might want to give it a light spritz of cooking spray. Nonstick pans are sometimes not 100 percent nonstick if they have been used a lot.

5. Shape

With floured hands, pick up the dough and ease it back onto the work surface in a somewhat even, rectangular shape. You will stretch and fold this slack dough into something equal to the width of your bread pan.

Following the shaping instructions on pages 43 to 44, with two floured hands, stretch the dough, simultaneously pulling it right and left (just spread your hands both ways at the same time to stretch out the dough) until it resists—two to three times its original width—and then fold the ends back over each other, creating a "packet" the width of your baking pan.

Brush off any loose flour from the top of the dough and do a roll-up motion from the bottom up or from top to bottom to form a tube of dough that's about the same width as your baking pan. Place the dough seam-up or seam-down into the pan; either way is fine.

6. Proof

Put the lid onto the pan and set in a warm place to rise. It will be ready to bake when the dough rises to about ¼ inch below the lid. If it's pressing into the lid, it's okay to go ahead and bake it.

Plan on baking the loaf about 1¼ hours after it is shaped, assuming a room temperature of about 70°F / 21°C. If your kitchen is warmer, it will be optimally proofed faster.

7. Preheat

About 45 minutes prior to baking, position a rack in the middle of the oven and preheat the oven to 450°F / 230°C.

8. Bake

Place the pan on the center of the oven rack. Turn down the heat to 425°F / 220°C and bake for 30 minutes. Then lower the temperature again to 375°F / 190°C and bake for another 30 minutes.

Remove the pan with oven mitts or thick kitchen towels, remove the lid, and carefully tilt the pan to turn the loaf out. Let the loaf cool on a rack, so air can circulate around it, for at least 1 hour before slicing; overnight is much better for this bread.

CORN (FLOUR) BREAD

Open pan or
Dutch oven

Do a Web search for "corn bread," and something like zero hits offer up a yeasted loaf of wheat-flour bread that has corn or corn flour—or both—in it. Safe to say, this recipe isn't your mama's cornbread—but it sure is good.

For my first attempt at this, I used some good-quality cornmeal that I had on hand. The problem was the cornmeal didn't hydrate enough in the dough, and the loaf came out a little bit gritty. This is kind of too bad, because there are some excellent heirloom cornmeals available on the market. If the cornmeal were soaked in water overnight or cooked ahead of time, it would soften up and could work, but I modified course and decided to give it a go with corn flour, basically a fine grind of cornmeal. Corn flour is harder to find, but it is out there. I want yellow or red corn flour for its color and flavor. If you have a home grist mill (or a Vitamix-style blender) and grind whole grains into flour, then the world's your oyster—you can use your favorite cornmeal and grind it down to a fine flour.

You may not always have the time or the ingredients to go whole hog with corny additions to this bread, so I've created two versions of this recipe. The basic is the simplest with just corn flour in it (it's good), while The Whole Shebang has fresh corn kernels, juiced corn kernels, cob broth, and roasted and ground corn husks in the dough. (See page 122 for condensed instructions for the latter.) The Whole Shebang is fun for a special occasion during the summer corn season, and it's worth the extra effort. Then there are the corn flakes—as a topping. This is slightly impractical, as the flakes tend to fall off in the rising and baking, but the baked loaf looks so cool that it's worth mentioning. More flakes come off when you slice it, so you may question the whole thing. Still, the loaf looks super-cool.

Grilled or toasted, slices of this corn bread are lovely as a base for buttered tartines with a layer of good ham or prosciutto; fried eggs; grilled and sliced peaches dripping with honey; or roasted chicken pieces covered in a lemony gravy. Toast with jam is a given. Or just plain corn bread and butter? It's peaches and cream to me.

THIS RECIPE MAKES 1 PAN LOAF OF A LITTLE MORE THAN 2 POUNDS.

First rise
2½ to 3½ hours at 70°F / 21°C room temperature. Faster if warmer,
slower if cooler. Also faster if using corn liquids instead of plain water.

Proof time
About 1 hour at 70°F / 21°C room temperature.

Bake
Preheat to 450°F / 230°C for 45 minutes, bake at 425°F / 220°C for about 50 minutes.

Sample schedule
Begin at 9:30 a.m., finish mixing at 10 a.m., shape into a loaf at 1 p.m.,
and bake at 2 p.m.

Ingredient	Quantity	Baker's Percentage
White bread flour	400 g / 2¾ cups + 2 tsp	100%
Corn flour*	175 g / 1½ cups + 1 tsp	44%
Water (80°F / 27°C)**	425 g / 1¾ cups + 1 tsp	106%
Corn kernels (optional)	175 g / 1 cup	44%
Corn husks, roasted and ground (optional)	5 g / ¼ cup	1.25%
Fine sea salt	14 g / 2¾ tsp	3.5%
Instant dried yeast	2 g / ½ tsp	0.5%
Levain (optional)	100 g / ½ cup	12.5% of total flour (if used)
Corn flakes (preferably unsweetened)***	50 g / 1⅔ cups	

* I only include flour that leavens in the 100% marker. These baker's percentages consider the corn flour as an additive ingredient. The 100 percent flour total is the white bread flour only. All other baker's percentages are calculated against the white bread flour.

** Or a combination of water, kernel juice, and cob broth.

*** Unsweetened corn flakes won't burn, but sweetened corn flakes might be a problem.

1. Autolyse

Measure 425 grams (80°F / 27°C) water (or combination water, cob broth, and kernel juice) into a 6-quart round tub or similar container. If you have a levain, add 100 grams from the refrigerator—you can weigh it directly into the dough tub with its liquid. Stir a bit with your fingers to loosen up the culture. Add 400 grams white bread flour and 175 grams corn flour. Add the corn kernels and ground husks (if using). Mix by hand just until incorporated.

Sprinkle 14 grams fine sea salt evenly across the top of the autolyse dough. Then sprinkle 2 grams instant dried yeast on top of that. Let them rest there, where they will partially dissolve.

Cover and let rest for 15 to 20 minutes.

2. Mix

Mix by hand, wetting your working hand before mixing so the dough doesn't stick to you. Reach underneath the dough and grab about one-fourth of it. Gently stretch this section and fold it over the top to the other side of the dough. Repeat three more times with the remaining dough until the salt and yeast are fully enclosed.

Use the pincer method to fully integrate the ingredients. Make five or six pincer cuts across the entire mass of dough. Then fold the dough over itself a few times. Repeat, alternately cutting and folding, until all the ingredients are fully integrated. Let the dough rest for a few minutes, then fold for another 30 seconds or until the dough tightens up. The whole process should take about 5 minutes. The target dough temperature at the end of the mix is 73° to 75°F / 23° to 24°C. Cover the tub and let the dough rise until the next fold.

3. Fold & First Rise

This dough needs two folds (see page 41). It's easiest to apply the folds during the first hour after mixing the dough. Apply the first fold about 10 minutes after mixing and the second when you see the dough spread out in the tub. If need be, it's okay to fold later; just be sure to leave it alone for the last hour of rising. (This dough will rise faster if you use kernel juice and cob broth. The corn liquids add sugars to the dough, which will make the yeast move faster.)

When the dough is two and a half to three times its original volume, 2½ to 3½ hours after the mix (depending on whether you used corn liquid or water in the dough), it's ready to be made up into a loaf and put into its pan. If you are using a 6-quart dough tub, the ideal point is when the edge of the dough has reached all the way up to the 2-quart line on the side of the tub, and the dough will be domed—not flattened, not collapsed. If you're not using a marked dough tub, you'll have to eyeball it. Use your best judgment.

4. Remove the Dough from Its Tub

Moderately flour a work surface about 12 inches wide. Flour your hands and sprinkle a bit of flour around the edges of the tub. Tip the tub slightly and gently work your floured free hand beneath the dough to loosen it from the bottom of the tub. Then turn the tub on its side and ease the dough out onto the work surface without pulling or tearing it.

Even if your bread pan is nonstick, you might want to give it a light spritz of cooking spray. Nonstick pans are sometimes not 100 percent nonstick if they have been used a lot.

5. Shape

With floured hands, pick up the dough and ease it back onto the work surface in a somewhat even, rectangular shape. You will stretch and fold this slack dough into something equal to the width of your bread pan.

Following the shaping instructions on pages 43 to 44, with two floured hands, stretch the dough, simultaneously pulling it right and left (just spread your hands both ways at the same time to stretch out the dough) until it resists—two to three times its original width—and then fold the ends back over each other, creating a "packet" the width of your baking pan.

Brush off any loose flour from the top of the dough and do a roll-up motion from the bottom up or from top to bottom to form a tube of dough that's about the same width as your baking pan.

If you like, you can add a thin layer of corn flakes to the bread pan before you place the shaped loaf and they will stick to the bread as it bakes. You'll get a crunchy bottom of corn flakes on each slice—totally up to you.

Place the dough seam-up into the pan. The seam is usually visible; it's the part of the rolled-up dough where the outer edges have joined to enclose the interior parts of the newly shaped loaf.

For a corn-flakes topping, use your hand to apply a thin film of water across the entire top of the loaf. Sprinkle corn flakes to cover the loaf and pat them down firmly. Some of these are going to pop off as the dough rises.

6. Proof

Place your bread pan in a nonperforated plastic bag, but do not make it tight at the top. Leave plenty of room for the dough to expand, a few inches, and tuck the bag under the pan. It doesn't need to be airtight. The point of the bag is to keep the dough from drying out during the next hour of proof time.

With my usual bread pan (8½ by 4½ by 2¾ inches), I like to see the dough rising a bit above the rim of the pan before baking, but you can't let it go too far above or it will collapse over the edge. If your pan is larger, the dough likely won't rise above its rim. See photos of perfect proofing on page 50.

Plan on baking the loaf about an hour after it is shaped, assuming a room temperature of about 70°F / 21°C. If your kitchen is warmer, it will be optimally proofed more quickly.

7. Preheat

About 45 minutes prior to baking, position a rack in the middle of the oven and preheat the oven to 450°F / 230°C.

8. Bake

Remove the pan from the plastic bag and place it on the center of the oven rack. Turn down the heat to 425°F / 220°C. You can put a baking sheet underneath your bread pan to catch the stray corn flakes that might pop off as the bread rises in the oven, but the pan will be blocking the heat from the bottom of the oven (most ovens heat from the bottom), so you should remove the pan once the bread has fully sprung—about 15 minutes into the bake. This will allow the bottom of the pan loaf—corn flakes and all—to fully bake and color.

Bake for 30 minutes, then check for even baking (give the pan a turn if the baking is uneven). Bake for another 20 minutes. Because this dough has more moisture than traditional pan loaves, it needs a longer time than you might think to bake the inside fully and to color the sides and give them enough strength to avoid post-bake collapse.

After 50 minutes, the top of the loaf should be a dark golden color. The sides should have a medium golden color and the bottom might be a little darker gold.

Remove the pan with oven mitts or thick kitchen towels and carefully tilt it to turn the loaf out. If the loaf doesn't pop right out, use a folded kitchen towel to firmly grab one edge of the pan with one hand and use the other hand to pry the loaf out. (Use more cooking spray next time.) Let the loaf cool on a rack, so air can circulate around it, for at least 30 minutes before slicing; 1 hour is better.

The Whole Shebang

When I had my bakery at Trifecta, I designed a corn croissant that we made during fresh-corn season. I wanted to use all parts of the corn, so we added fresh corn kernels, hydrated the dough with juice from fresh kernels that we ran through a juicer, and made a concentrated broth from the leftover cobs by simply boiling them in enough water to cover and reducing the water to a small amount. We roasted the corn husks in the bread oven until they got pretty dark, ground them in a coffee grinder, and then tossed them into the dough. After the corn croissants came out of the oven, we put a bourbon glaze on half of them, because *corn*. Here are shorthand instructions for The Whole Shebang corn bread, made with the same approach except the glaze. Just drink the bourbon.

Position a rack in the middle of the oven and preheat the oven to 500°F / 260°C.

Remove the husks from an ear of corn and place them on a baking sheet or in a cast-iron skillet. Put the pan on the oven rack and roast the husks until very dark brown and nearly charred, 10 to 12 minutes. Remove from the oven and let cool. Then break the husks into pieces small enough to fit into a food processor or coffee or spice grinder. Process until you have a coarse husk flour made up of pieces and flakes the size of rough sand and a little bigger. Set aside.

Cut the kernels from 3 or 4 ears of corn and juice them, or run through a blender and strain the juice. Set aside.

Break the spent corncobs in half, put them into a large pot, add water to cover, and boil until about ½ cup cob broth remains.

Measure the fresh corn juice and cob broth into a container to make up 425 grams / 1¾ cups + 1 tsp liquid for the dough mix.

Follow the recipe directions, substituting the corn liquid for the water, and add about 5 grams / ¼ cup of the roasted corn husk flour to the autolyse mix.

Pay close attention to the pace of the dough rising. The sugars in the corn broth and kernel juice will accelerate the rise of the dough.

RAISIN-PECAN BREAD

Open pan, lidded pan,
or Dutch oven

This is an easy open-pan version of the raisin-pecan bread that we make daily at Ken's Artisan Bakery. That one is a pure levain bread. We make up loaves into 400-gram torpedoes, crosshatch the scoring, and bake at a high temperature with a blast of steam until the tips start to turn black. You could also bake this as a Dutch-oven loaf, or you can convert it to an overnight cold-proof bread that you bake in the morning. Check out the instructions on page 150.

Significant to this recipe is that the raisins are soaked in Earl Grey tea overnight—or for at least a couple of hours—in advance of mixing them into the dough. The raisin soaking liquid goes into the dough, too, so don't toss it.

I think this bread wants to be toasted and spread with the best butter you can buy or a fresh, soft cheese. Don't complicate it. There's enough complexity in the bread itself. It would go very well with charcuterie, or butter and ham. If you want to make tapas with this, try topping quartered slices with scrambled eggs or slices from a Japanese rolled omelet that is cooked tamagoyaki-style. I originally developed this bread to go with a cheese plate at long-gone Portland restaurant Fenouil. We sell it at my shop to this day. It's hard to stop eating it. Tea it up!

THIS RECIPE MAKES 1 PAN LOAF OF ABOUT 2 POUNDS.

First rise

3 hours at 70°F / 21°C room temperature. Faster if warmer, slower if cooler.

Proof time

About 1 hour at 70°F / 21°C room temperature.

Bake

Preheat to 450°F / 230°C for 45 minutes,
bake at 425°F / 220°C for about 50 minutes.

Sample schedule

Soak the raisins in Earl Grey tea for at least 2 hours or preferably overnight
before you mix your dough. Then begin your dough mix at 9:30 a.m., finish
mixing at 10 a.m., shape into a loaf at 1 p.m. and bake at 2 p.m.

Ingredient	Quantity	Baker's Percentage
White bread flour	375 g / 2⅔ cups + 1½ tsp	75%
Rye flour	75 g / ½ cup + 1 Tbsp + ¾ tsp	15%
Whole-wheat flour	50 g / ⅓ cup + 1¼ tsp	10%
Water (90° to 95°F / 32° to 35°C) and soaking liquid, 50-50*	370 g / 1½ cups + 2 tsp	74%
Fine sea salt	12 g / scant 2½ tsp	2.4%
Instant dried yeast	3 g / 1 tsp	0.6%
Levain (optional)	100 g / ½ cup	9% of total flour (if used)
Raisins*	100 g / ½ cup + 3 Tbsp + 1¼ tsp	20%
Chopped pecans	80 g / ½ cup + 2 Tbsp	16%
Earl Grey tea*	335 g / 1½ cups	

* *The night before you make dough, or at least 2 hours ahead of time, make about 1½ cups Earl Grey
tea and add the raisins to the tea. Let them soak at room temperature until you are ready to mix the
dough, then strain, reserving the soaking liquid for using in the dough mix.*

1. Autolyse

Measure 185 grams of the (room-temperature) Earl Grey tea remaining from soaking the raisins and 185 grams (90° to 95°F / 32° to 35°C) water into a 6-quart round tub or similar container. If you have a levain, add 100 grams from the refrigerator—you can weigh it directly into the dough tub with its liquid. Stir a bit with your fingers to loosen up the culture. Add 375 grams white bread flour, 75 grams rye flour, and 50 grams whole-wheat flour. Then add the tea-soaked raisins, well drained or squeezed of excess liquid. Mix it by hand until all is incorporated.

Sprinkle 12 grams fine sea salt evenly across the top of the autolyse dough. Then sprinkle 3 grams instant dried yeast on top of that. Let them rest there, where they will partially dissolve.

Cover and let rest for 15 to 20 minutes. Measure out 80 grams chopped pecans so they will be on hand when you need them.

2. Mix

Mix by hand, wetting your working hand before mixing so the dough doesn't stick to you. Reach underneath the dough and grab about one-fourth of it. Gently stretch this section and fold it over the top to the other side of the dough. Repeat three more times with the remaining dough until the salt and yeast are fully enclosed. (You'll notice the rye dough doesn't stretch as much as the doughs made with just wheat flour.)

Use the pincer method to fully integrate the ingredients. Make five or six pincer cuts across the entire mass of dough. Then fold the dough over itself a few times. Repeat, alternately cutting and folding, until all the ingredients are fully integrated. Add the pecan pieces and use the same pincer method—cut and fold—to integrate the nuts more or less evenly throughout the dough. Let the dough rest for a few minutes, then fold for another 30 seconds or until the dough tightens up. The whole process should take about 5 minutes. The target dough temperature at the end of the mix is 73° to 75°F / 23° to 24°C. Cover the tub and let the dough rise until the next fold.

3. Fold & First Rise

This dough needs two folds (see page 41). It's easiest to apply the folds during the first hour after mixing the dough. Apply the first fold about 10 minutes after mixing and the second when you see the dough spread out in the tub. If need be, it's okay to fold later; just be sure to leave it alone for the last hour of rising.

When the dough is two and a half to three times its original volume, about 3 hours after the mix, it's ready to be made up into a loaf and put into its pan. If you are using a 6-quart dough tub, the ideal point is when the edge of the dough has reached all the way up the 2-quart line on the side of the tub, and the dough will be domed—not flattened, not collapsed. It'll be best if you don't let it go beyond that, as you want to preserve what's left of the rise for the next stage, in the pan. If you're not using a marked dough tub, you'll have to eyeball it. Use your best judgment.

4. Remove the Dough from Its Tub

Lightly flour a work surface about 12 inches wide. Flour your hands and sprinkle a bit of flour around the edges of the dough. Tip the tub slightly and gently work your floured free hand beneath the dough to loosen it from the bottom of the tub. Then turn the tub on its side and ease the dough out onto the work surface without pulling or tearing it.

Even if your bread pan is nonstick, you might want to give it a light spritz of cooking spray. Nonstick pans are sometimes not 100 percent nonstick if they have been used a lot.

5. Shape

With floured hands, pick up the dough and ease it back onto the work surface in a somewhat even, rectangular shape. You will stretch and fold this slack dough into something equal to the width of your bread pan.

Following the shaping instructions on pages 43 to 44, with two floured hands, stretch the dough, simultaneously pulling it right and left (just spread your hands both ways at the same time to stretch out the dough) until it resists—two to three times its original width—and then fold the ends back over each other, creating a "packet" the width of your baking pan.

Brush off any loose flour from the top of the dough and do a roll-up motion from the bottom up or from top to bottom to form a tube of dough that's about the same width as your baking pan. Place the dough seam up into the pan. The seam is usually visible; it's the part of the rolled-up dough where the outer edges have joined to enclose the interior parts of the newly shaped loaf.

6. Proof

Use your hand to apply a light film of water across the entire top surface of the dough after it's in its pan. Then place your bread pan in a nonperforated plastic bag, but do not make it tight at the top. Leave plenty of room for the dough to expand, a few inches, and tuck the bag under the pan. It doesn't need to be airtight. The point of the bag is to keep the dough from drying out during the next hour of proof time.

With my usual bread pan (8½ by 4½ by 2¾ inches), I like to see the dough rising a bit above the rim of the pan before baking, but you can't let it go too far above or it will collapse over the edge. If your pan is larger, the dough likely won't rise above its rim. See photos of perfect proofing on page 50.

Plan on baking the loaf about an hour after it is shaped, assuming a room temperature of about 70°F / 21°C. If your kitchen is warmer, it will be optimally proofed earlier.

7. Preheat

About 45 minutes prior to baking, position a rack in the middle of the oven and preheat the oven to 450°F / 230°C.

8. Bake

Remove the pan from the plastic bag and place it on the center of the oven rack. Turn down the heat to 425°F / 220°C and bake. After 30 minutes, check for even baking (give the pan a turn if the baking is uneven) and bake for another 20 minutes. Because this dough has more water than traditional pan loaves, it needs a longer time than you might think to bake the inside fully and to color the sides and give them enough strength to avoid post-bake collapse.

After 50 minutes, the top of the loaf should be darkly colored (use the photo on page 124 as a reference). The sides and bottom should not be as dark as the top.

Remove the pan with oven mitts or thick kitchen towels and carefully tilt it to turn the loaf out. If a hard rap on the counter doesn't free the loaf, use a folded kitchen towel to firmly grab one edge of the pan with one hand and use your other hand to pry the loaf out. (Use more cooking spray next time.) Let the loaf cool on a rack, so air can circulate around it, for at least 30 minutes before slicing; 1 hour is better.

HAZELNUT BREAD

Open pan, lidded pan, or Dutch oven

Hazelnuts used to be better known as *filberts* in Oregon. This recipe uses hazelnut meal in the dough and has no sugar or dairy, which is atypical of a baked good containing nut meal. Ground nut meal (freshly ground is by far the best) has the consistency of fatty, very coarse flour. You can buy excellent freshly ground hazelnut meal online (if you are in a store, check the package date and shelf life before you buy), but it may be easier to buy whole hazelnuts and grind them yourself. They are fairly soft and can easily be ground in a food processor, though you need to be careful not to overprocess and turn them into nut butter. If you buy raw hazelnuts, roast them gently before grinding. You can roughly rub the roasted nuts in a coarse dish towel to remove some of their brown skin, but it's not necessary to obsess over removing all of it. We have been using Oregon's Freddy Guys hazelnuts and hazelnut meal at my bakery for almost twenty years in pastry: hazelnut butter cookies and a hazelnut tart, for example. This recipe is based on The Standard loaf (see page 81), with the addition of hazelnut meal and crushed or cracked nuts.

Most nut breads, like my walnut breads, add whole nuts or nut pieces to the dough. I use ground nuts along with nut pieces in this recipe because it completely integrates the flavor of the nuts and their oil. You get more than just nut bites in the bread—the entire loaf is nutty. It's pretty great. You could also use almond meal (commonly used in pastry, but almonds are harder than hazelnuts and thus more difficult to grind) and almond pieces instead of hazelnuts. Walnuts, peanuts, or cashews could be ground and used as a one-for-one replacement too.

Make soft-boiled or scrambled eggs or brown sugar–baked beans and serve them on buttered hazelnut toast. Use this bread to make savory croutons to go on a simple green salad. Toast with butter, honey, and blue cheese, please. Try a sliced pear and goat cheese sandwich on this bread.

When this bakes, your house will smell like a fragrant memory of a dream of a perfect place.

THIS RECIPE MAKES 1 PAN LOAF OF ABOUT 2 POUNDS.

First rise
3 to 3½ hours at 70°F / 21°C room temperature.
Faster if warmer, slower if cooler.

Proof time
About 1 hour at 70°F / 21°C room temperature.

Bake
Preheat to 450°F / 230°C for 45 minutes,
bake at 425°F / 220°C for about 50 minutes.

Sample schedule
Begin at 9:30 a.m., finish mixing at 10 a.m., shape into a loaf at 1:30 p.m.,
and bake at 2:30 p.m.

Ingredient	Quantity	Baker's Percentage
White bread flour	400 g / 2¾ cups + 2 tsp	80%
Whole-wheat flour	100 g / ½ cup + 3 Tbsp + 1¼ tsp	20%
Water (90° to 95°F / 32° to 35°C)	420 g / 1½ cups + 3 Tbsp + 2 tsp	84%
Fine sea salt	12 g / scant 2½ tsp	2.4%
Instant dried yeast	3 g / 1 tsp	0.6%
Levain (optional)	100 g / ½ cup	9% of total flour (if used)
Hazelnut meal	75 g / ½ cup + 2 Tbsp	15%
Roasted hazelnuts*	75 g / ½ cup + 2 Tbsp	15%

* Buy whole roasted hazelnuts and crack them yourself; see Step 1b.

1a. Autolyse

Measure 420 grams (90° to 95°F / 32° to 35°C) water into a 6-quart round tub or similar container. If you have a levain, add 100 grams from the refrigerator—you can weigh it directly into the dough tub with its water. Stir a bit with your fingers to loosen up the culture. Add 400 grams white bread flour, 100 grams whole-wheat flour, and 75 grams hazelnut meal. Mix it by hand until all is incorporated.

Sprinkle 12 grams fine sea salt evenly across the top of the autolyse dough. Then sprinkle 3 grams instant dried yeast on top of that. Let them rest there, where they will partially dissolve.

Cover and let rest for 15 to 20 minutes.

1b. Crack the Whole Hazelnuts

Hazelnuts are soft nuts and split or crack very easily if roasted. I give each—one at a time—a soft, downward crack on a hard surface with my palm. The harder you hit, the more pieces the nut will break into. I like to tap just hard enough to split them into two pieces. Set aside.

2. Mix

Mix by hand, wetting your working hand before mixing so the dough doesn't stick to you. Reach underneath the dough and grab about one-fourth of it. Gently stretch this section and fold it over the top to the other side of the dough. Repeat three more times with the remaining dough until the salt and yeast are fully enclosed.

Use the pincer method to fully integrate the ingredients. Make five or six pincer cuts across the entire mass of dough. Then fold the dough over itself a few times. Repeat, alternately cutting and folding, until all the ingredients are fully integrated. Add 75 grams hazelnut pieces and use the same pincer method—cut and fold—to integrate the nuts more or less evenly throughout the dough. Let the dough rest for a few minutes, then fold for another 30 seconds or until the dough tightens up. The whole process should take about 5 minutes. The target dough temperature at the end of the mix is 75° to 78°F / 24° to 26°C. Cover the tub and let the dough rise until the next fold.

3. Fold & First Rise

This dough needs just one fold (see page 41). It's easiest to apply the fold during the first hour after mixing the dough.

When the dough is two and a half to three times its original volume, about 3½ hours after the mix, it's ready to be made up into a loaf and put into its pan. If you are using a 6-quart dough tub, the ideal point is when the edge of the dough has reached all the way up to the 2-quart line on the side of the tub, and the dough will be slightly domed—not flattened, not collapsed. If it reaches a little above the 2-quart line on your dough tub, that's fine too. It'll be best if you don't let it go beyond that, as you want to preserve what's left of the rise for the next stage, in the pan. If the room is cool and the dough is taking longer, let the dough continue to rise until it reaches this amount of volume expansion. If you're not using a marked dough tub, you'll have to eyeball it. Use your best judgment.

4. Remove the Dough from Its Tub

Lightly flour a work surface about 12 inches wide. Flour your hands and sprinkle a bit of flour around the edges of the tub. Tip the tub slightly and gently work your floured free hand beneath the dough to loosen it from the bottom of the tub. Then turn the tub on its side and ease the dough out onto the work surface without pulling or tearing it.

Even if your bread pan is nonstick, you might want to give it a light spritz of cooking spray. Nonstick pans are sometimes not 100 percent nonstick if they have been used a lot.

5. Shape

With floured hands, pick up the dough and ease it back onto the work surface in a somewhat even, rectangular shape. You will stretch and fold this slack dough into something equal to the width of your bread pan.

Following the shaping instructions on pages 43 to 44, with two floured hands, stretch the dough, simultaneously pulling it right and left (just spread your hands both ways at the same time to stretch out the dough) until it resists—two to three times its original width—and then fold the ends back over each other, creating a "packet" the width of your baking pan.

Brush off any loose flour from the top of the dough and do a roll-up motion from the bottom up or from top to bottom to form a tube of dough that's about the same width as your baking pan. Place the dough seam-up into the pan. The seam is usually visible; it's the part of the rolled-up dough where the outer edges have joined to enclose the interior parts of the newly shaped loaf.

6. Proof

Use your hand to apply a light film of water across the entire top surface of the dough after it's in its pan. Then place your bread pan in a nonperforated plastic bag, but do not make it tight at the top. Leave plenty of room for the dough to expand, a few inches, and tuck the bag under the pan. It doesn't need to be airtight. The point of the bag is to keep the dough from drying out during the next hour of proof time.

With my usual bread pan (8½ by 4½ by 2¾ inches), I like to see the dough rising a bit above the rim of the pan before baking, but you can't let it go too far above or it will collapse over the edge. If your pan is larger, the dough likely won't rise above its rim. See photos of perfect proofing on page 50.

Plan on baking the loaf about an hour after it is shaped, assuming a room temperature of about 70°F / 21°C. If your kitchen is warmer, it will be optimally proofed earlier.

7. Preheat

About 45 minutes prior to baking, position a rack in the middle of the oven and preheat the oven to 450°F / 230°C.

8. Bake

Remove the pan from the plastic bag and place it on the center of the oven rack. Turn down the heat to 425°F / 220°C and bake. After 30 minutes, check for even baking (give the pan a turn if the baking is uneven) and bake for another 20 minutes. Because this dough has more water than traditional pan loaves, it needs a longer time than you might think to bake the inside fully and to color the sides and give them enough strength to avoid post-bake collapse.

After 50 minutes, the top of the loaf should be darkly colored (use the photo on page 130 as a reference). The sides and bottom should not be as dark as the top.

Remove the pan with oven mitts or thick kitchen towels and carefully tilt it to turn the loaf out. If a hard rap on the counter doesn't free the loaf, use a folded kitchen towel to firmly grab one edge of the pan with one hand and use your other hand to pry the loaf out. (Use more cooking spray next time.) Let the loaf cool on a rack, so air can circulate around it, for at least 30 minutes before slicing; 1 hour is better.

MULTIGRAIN BREAD

Open pan or
Dutch oven

Multigrain bread is the ultimate "bread with stuff in it" recipe. In recent years, it has been popularized as a good-for-you product, but many of the shelf-stable varieties that you find are enhanced with added gluten, sweeteners, and preservatives so they will last a week on store shelves.

You'll find none of those in my take, but instead rolled oats, rolled barley, and buckwheat groats. Using 120 grams of only one grain, like rolled heirloom barley, is a simple and good option too. The possibilities are endless, and that's part of the fun. You can make a roll-your-own multigrain blend using a variety of cereals that you may already have in your pantry. This is sort of the kitchen sink of breads. Quinoa is an option, and so is leftover rice; cooked black rice or wild rice can work. Add nuts if you want, but try to use some restraint: this recipe doesn't need a thousand things in it. While I make this as a pan bread, it works great as a Dutch-oven bread too.

The dried grains—in this case, the rolled barley, rolled oats, and buckwheat groats—need to be soaked from between 6 hours to overnight before they go into the dough. (A shorter soak gives buckwheat groats a little bit of "tooth," which I discovered that I like.) One key to this recipe is using the soaking liquid in the dough. It has a milky color and tastes mildly of the grains. I like to top the bread with rolled oats because they look nice. The other key is using the best-quality ingredients, as always. Some craft farms offer heirloom varieties of barley that are delicious. For example, Purple Karma barley flakes from Camas Country Mill are from an ancient Himalayan landrace variety.

Many whole grains have a mildly bitter flavor from their bran (the outer layer of the berry). It is customary to include a sweetener in multigrain bread doughs to offset that bitterness. I use a small amount of honey in this recipe. You could also add a little bit of brown sugar, or use no sweetener at all. If you remove the sweetener, the dough may take a little longer to rise, so please pay attention to the recipe notes describing how much rise is needed.

First rise

3 to 3½ hours at 70°F / 21°C room temperature. Faster if warmer, slower if cooler.

Proof time

About 1½ hours at 70°F / 21°C room temperature.

Bake

Preheat to 450°F / 230°C for 45 minutes, bake at 425°F / 220°C for 55 to 60 minutes.

Sample schedule

Begin at 9:30 a.m., finish mixing at 10 a.m., shape into a loaf at 1:30 p.m., and bake at 3 p.m.

Ingredient	Quantity	Baker's Percentage
White bread flour	280 g / 2 cups	70%
Whole-wheat or whole-spelt flour*	120 g / ¾ cup + 2 Tbsp + 2¼ tsp	30%
Water (90° to 95°F / 32° to 35°C)	70 g / ¼ cup + 2 tsp	17.5%
Barley/oat/buckwheat soaking liquid (about 70°F / 21°C)	225 g / ¾ cup + 3 Tbsp	56.25%
Fine sea salt	14 g / 2¾ tsp	3.5%
Instant dried yeast	3 g / 1 tsp	0.75%
Honey	15 g / 2 tsp	3.75%
Buckwheat groats	40 g / 3 Tbsp + 1¾ tsp	10%
Rolled barley	40 g / ¼ cup + 2 Tbsp + 1¼ tsp	10%
Rolled oats (for the dough)	40 g / ¼ cup + 2 Tbsp + 1¼ tsp	10%
Rolled oats (for topping the loaf)	15 g / 2 Tbsp + 1¼ tsp	
Levain (optional)	100 g / ½ cup	9% of total flour (if used)

* *Any whole-grain heritage wheat will work.*

1a. Soak the Grains

The night before you want to bake (or 6 to 8 hours soak time, if you want a little more texture), measure 40 grams each of the buckwheat groats, rolled barley, and rolled oats (or 120 grams of just one) into a container and cover with cold water. Let it sit out overnight at room temperature.

The next morning, strain the soaked grains through a fine-mesh strainer set over a bowl and firmly press against the grains to remove as much liquid as possible. Reserve the soaking liquid for the dough.

1b. Autolyse

Measure 225 grams of the soaking liquid into a 6-quart round tub or similar container. Add 70 grams (90° to 95°F / 32° to 35°C) water. If you have a levain, add 100 grams from the refrigerator—you can weigh it directly into the dough tub with its water. Stir a bit with your fingers to loosen up the culture. Add 280 grams white bread flour and 120 grams whole-wheat or whole-spelt flour. Add all the soaked grains. Mix it by hand until all is incorporated. It's going to be a pretty wet dough, so don't worry about that.

Put 2 teaspoons honey on one side of the top of the dough and sprinkle 14 grams fine sea salt evenly across the other side. Then sprinkle 3 grams instant dried yeast on top of the salt. Let them rest there, where they will partially dissolve.

Cover and let rest for 15 to 20 minutes.

2. Mix

Mix by hand, wetting your working hand before mixing so the dough doesn't stick to you. Reach underneath the dough and grab about one-fourth of it. Gently stretch this section and fold it over the top to the other side of the dough. Repeat three more times with the remaining dough until the salt and yeast are fully enclosed.

Use the pincer method to fully integrate the ingredients. Make five or six pincer cuts across the entire mass of dough. Then fold the dough over itself a few times. Repeat, alternately cutting and folding, until all the ingredients are fully integrated. The whole process should take about 5 minutes. The target dough temperature at the end of the mix is about 68°F / 20°C. This dough mixes cooler because of the room-temperature soaking liquid (I'm assuming the dough will be 65° to 70°F / 18° to 21°C). Cover the tub and let the dough rise until the next fold. The rise time will be on a par with the other pan-bread recipes in this book even though the dough is cooler because the soaking liquid and the honey provide additional food for the yeast. This dough will rise very nicely.

3. Fold & First Rise

This dough needs two folds (see page 41). It's easiest to apply the folds during the first hour after mixing the dough. Apply the first fold about 10 minutes after mixing and the second after you see the dough spread out in the tub. If need be, it's okay to fold later; just be sure to leave it alone for the last hour of rising.

When the dough is two and a half to three times its original volume, about 3 hours after the mix, it's ready to be made up into a loaf and put into its pan. If you are using a 6-quart dough tub, the ideal point is when the edge of the dough has reached just shy (about ¼ inch) of the 2-quart line on the side of the tub, and the dough will be slightly domed—not flattened, not collapsed. If it reaches the 2-quart line on your dough tub, that's fine too. It'll be best if you don't let it go beyond that, as you want to preserve what's left of the rise for the next stage, in the pan. If the room is cool and the dough is taking longer, let the dough continue to rise until it reaches this amount of volume expansion. If you're not using a marked dough tub, you'll have to eyeball it. Use your best judgment.

4. Remove the Dough from Its Tub

Lightly flour a work surface about 12 inches wide. Flour your hands and sprinkle a bit of flour around the edges of the tub. Tip the tub slightly and gently work your floured free hand beneath the dough to loosen it from the bottom of the tub. Then turn the tub on its side and ease the dough out onto the work surface without pulling or tearing it.

Even if your bread pan is nonstick, you might want to give it a light spritz of cooking spray. Nonstick pans are sometimes not 100 percent nonstick if they have been used a lot.

5. Shape

With floured hands, pick up the dough and ease it back onto the work surface in a somewhat even, rectangular shape. You will stretch and fold this slack dough into something equal to the width of your bread pan.

Following the shaping instructions on pages 43 to 44, with two floured hands, stretch the dough, simultaneously pulling it right and left (just spread your hands both ways at the same time to stretch out the dough) until it resists—two to three times its original width—and then fold the ends back over each other, creating a "packet" the width of your baking pan.

Brush off any loose flour from the top of the dough and do a roll-up motion from the bottom up or from top to bottom to form a tube of dough that's about the same width as your baking pan. Place the dough seam-up into the pan. The seam is usually visible; it's the part of the rolled-up dough where the outer edges have joined to enclose the interior parts of the newly shaped loaf.

For a rolled-oats topping, apply a thin film of water with your hand to cover the entire top of the loaf. Sprinkle 15 grams oats to cover the loaf and pat them down firmly.

6. Proof

Place your bread pan in a nonperforated plastic bag, but do not make it tight at the top. Leave plenty of room for the dough to expand, a few inches, and tuck the bag under the pan. It doesn't need to be airtight. The point of the bag is to keep the dough from drying out during the next 1½ hours of proof time.

With my usual bread pan (8½ by 4½ by 2¾ inches), I like to see the dough rising a bit above the rim of the pan before baking, but you can't let it go too far above or it will collapse over the edge. If your pan is larger, the dough likely won't rise above its rim. See photos of perfect proofing on page 50.

Plan on baking the loaf about 1½ hours after it is shaped, assuming a room temperature of about 70°F / 21°C. If your kitchen is warmer, the bread will be optimally proofed more quickly. This loaf only needs to rise to the top of the pan before baking; it will get a generous spring in the oven.

7. Preheat

About 45 minutes prior to baking, position a rack in the middle of the oven and preheat the oven to 450°F / 230°C.

8. Bake

Remove the pan from the plastic bag and place it on the center of the oven rack. Turn down the heat to 425°F / 220°C and bake. After 30 minutes, check for even baking (give the pan a turn if the baking is uneven) and bake for another 25 to 30 minutes. Because this dough has more water than traditional pan loaves, it needs a longer time than you might think to fully bake the inside and to color the sides and give them enough strength to avoid post-bake collapse.

Bake until the top of the loaf is very dark. This bread takes a little longer to bake than the other pan loaves—about 1 hour instead of 50 minutes. Pay close attention to the final 10 minutes of the bake; the sides and bottom should not be as dark as the top.

Remove the pan with oven mitts or thick kitchen towels and carefully tilt it to turn the loaf out. If a hard rap on the counter doesn't free the loaf, use a folded kitchen towel to firmly grab one edge of the pan with one hand and use your other hand to pry the loaf out. (Use more cooking spray next time.) Let the loaf cool on a rack, so air can circulate around it, for at least 30 minutes before slicing; 1 hour is better.

CHAPTER 5
OVERNIGHT COLD-PROOF RECIPES

These loaves spend the night in the refrigerator and are ready to bake first thing in the morning, 10 to 14 hours after they were made up the previous evening. They will have a slightly more complex flavor than a same-day bread with the same amount of effort. The extra ingredient is time. Thrill your family, your housemates, or your dog with the smell of baking bread to go with morning coffee.

You can easily convert any of the same-day loaves to an overnight cold-proof loaf if that suits your schedule better (see instructions on page 150). The overnight cold proof gives time for a more substantial secondary fermentation to develop than what happens in the same-day bread doughs. You'll get a little more depth of flavor and maybe another day of shelf life. The extended cold fermentation lends itself especially well to New York–Style Rye Bread with Caraway, which is a home version of a deli-style rye bread. The 100% Spelt Pan Bread introduces you to the lovely flavors from this third ancient grain.

THE STANDARD #2

Open pan, lidded pan, or Dutch oven

This version of The Standard loaf has you cold proof the dough overnight in the refrigerator to be baked the next morning. It's a great way to start your day, and I've repeated this one recipe with complete instructions to show you how to adapt any same-day recipe to an overnight cold-proof recipe.

I like the classic look of bread slices from a loaf that has spread-out "ears" where its top has expanded both up and sideways during its rise and then more in the oven. You can get the ears with the same-day loaf, but the timing needs to be more precise. The cold dough has added strength because colder temperatures tighten up the gluten, even as the loaf expands.

You might just do the overnight cold proof because the schedule suits you, as it's a convenient one. If you want to bake at 9 a.m., for example, you would want to mix the dough around 6 p.m. the day before. Three hours later, you'll make up the loaf, cover it, and put it into the fridge. In the morning, preheat the oven, then bake.

There is just a little less water in this recipe than in the same-day loaf, and the timing is adjusted too. Less water adds a bit more strength to the dough and minimizes its tendency to droop too much over the sides of the bread pan while it very slowly rises in the refrigerator. My early tests saw the dough doing a Dalí-esque clock flop way over the rim of the pan when I removed it from the fridge to bake the next morning. If this happens to you, go ahead and bake it. You'll have a crunchy snack to peel off, and the rest of the loaf will be fine. But next time, cut back on the amount of time in the first rise, before you make up the loaf, and judge by volume expansion: about ½ inch below the 2-quart line if you are using a dough tub with volume markings on the side. It moves pretty fast during the last 30 minutes of its first rise.

Feel free to sub any whole-grain stone-milled specialty-wheat flour of your choice in place of the whole-wheat flour in this recipe.

THIS RECIPE MAKES 1 PAN LOAF OF ABOUT 2 POUNDS.

First rise
About 3 hours at 70°F / 21°C room temperature.
Faster if warmer, slower if cooler.

Proof time
10 to 14 hours in the refrigerator.

Bake
Preheat to 450°F / 230°C for 45 minutes,
bake at 425°F / 220°C for about 50 minutes.

Sample schedule
Begin at 6 p.m., finish mixing at 6:30 p.m., shape into a loaf at 9:30 p.m.,
and bake at 9 a.m. the next day.

Ingredient	Quantity	Baker's Percentage
White bread flour	400 g / 2¾ cups + 2 tsp	80%
Whole-wheat flour	100 g / ½ cup + 3 Tbsp + 1¼ tsp	20%
Water (90° to 95°F / 32° to 35°C)	380 g / 1½ cups + 1 Tbsp + 1 tsp	76%
Fine sea salt	11 g / 2¼ tsp	2.2%
Instant dried yeast	3 g / 1 tsp	0.6%
Levain (optional)	100 g / ½ cup	9% of total flour (if used)

1. Autolyse

Measure 380 grams (90° to 95°F / 32° to 35°C) water into a 6-quart round tub or similar container. If you have a levain, add 100 grams from the refrigerator—you can weigh it directly into the dough tub with its water. Stir a bit with your fingers to loosen up the culture. Add 400 grams white bread flour and 100 grams whole-wheat flour. Mix it by hand until all is incorporated.

Sprinkle 11 grams fine sea salt evenly across the top of the autolyse dough. Then sprinkle 3 grams instant dried yeast on top of that. Let them rest there, where they will partially dissolve.

Cover and let rest for 15 to 20 minutes.

2. Mix

Mix by hand, wetting your working hand before mixing so the dough doesn't stick to you. Reach underneath the dough and grab about one-fourth of it. Gently stretch this section and fold it over the top to the other side of the dough. Repeat three more times with the remaining dough until the salt and yeast are fully enclosed.

Use the pincer method to fully integrate the ingredients. Make five or six pincer cuts across the entire mass of dough. Then fold the dough over itself a few times. Repeat, alternately cutting and folding, until all the ingredients are fully integrated. Let the dough rest for a few minutes, then fold for another 30 seconds or until the dough tightens up. The whole process should take about 5 minutes. The target dough temperature at the end of the mix is about 75°F / 24°C. Cover the tub and let the dough rise until the next fold.

3. Fold & First Rise

This dough needs three folds (see page 41), one more than the same-day Standard loaf, to give it a little more strength to handle the long overnight rise in the refrigerator. Apply the first fold about 10 minutes after mixing and the second and third when you see the dough spread out in the tub from the previous fold. If need be, it's okay to fold later; just be sure to leave it alone for the last hour of rising.

When the dough is about two and a half times its original volume, about 3 hours after the mix, it's ready to be made up into a loaf and put into its pan. If you are using a 6-quart dough tub, the ideal point is when the edge of the dough has reached about 1/2 inch below the 2-quart line on the side of the tub, and the dough will be domed—not flattened, not collapsed. If it reaches the 2-quart line on your dough tub, you have caught it a little late, but you can lightly punch down the dough and de-gas it before shaping it into a loaf. Compared to the same-day dough this gets a little less rise in the first rise, which gets the dough into the refrigerator about 30 minutes earlier. Otherwise, the dough might rise over the edges of the pan. If the room is cool and the dough is taking longer, let it continue to rise until it reaches this amount of volume expansion. If you're not using a marked dough tub, you'll have to eyeball it. Use your best judgment.

4. Remove the Dough from Its Tub

Lightly flour a work surface about 12 inches wide. Flour your hands and sprinkle a bit of flour around the edges of the tub. Tip the tub slightly and gently work your floured free hand beneath the dough to loosen it from the bottom of the tub. Then turn the tub on its side and ease the dough out onto the work surface without pulling or tearing it.

Even if your bread pan is nonstick, you might want to give it a light spritz of cooking spray. Nonstick pans are sometimes not 100 percent nonstick if they have been used a lot.

5. Shape

With floured hands, pick up the dough and ease it back onto the work surface in a somewhat even, rectangular shape. You will stretch and fold this slack dough into something equal to the width of your bread pan.

Following the shaping instructions on pages 43 to 44, with two floured hands, stretch the dough, simultaneously pulling it right and left (just spread your hands both ways at the same time to stretch out the dough) until it resists—two to three times its original width—and then fold the ends back over each other, creating a "packet" the width of your baking pan.

Brush off any loose flour from the top of the dough and do a roll-up motion from the bottom up or from top to bottom to form a tube of dough that's about the same width as your baking pan. Place the dough seam-up into the pan. The seam is usually visible; it's the part of the rolled-up dough where the outer edges have joined to enclose the interior parts of the newly shaped loaf.

6. Proof

Use your hand to apply a light film of water across the entire top surface of the dough after it's in its pan. This prevents the dough from sticking to its proofing bag as it expands in the refrigerator overnight.

Lightly punch down the dough to de-gas it a bit. Then place your bread pan in a nonperforated plastic bag, but do not make it tight at the top. Leave plenty of room for the dough to expand, a few inches, and tuck the bag under the pan. Put the pan into the refrigerator.

The next morning, the dough should have inflated above the pan line if you are using the USA Pan that measures 8½ by 4½ by 2¾ inches. It might look like too much! No fear. A little bit of droop over the edges is desirable, and it should look domed in the middle. In a larger bread pan, it is less likely the dough will rise above the pan line. See photos of a perfect proofing on page 50.

7. Preheat

About 45 minutes prior to baking, position a rack in the middle of the oven and preheat the oven to 450°F / 230°C.

8. Bake

Remove the pan from the plastic bag and place it on the center of the oven rack. Turn down the heat to 425°F / 220°C and bake. After 30 minutes, check for even baking (give the pan a turn if the baking is uneven) and bake for another 20 minutes. Because this dough has more water than traditional pan loaves, it needs a longer time than you might think to bake the inside fully and to color the sides and give them enough strength to avoid post-bake collapse.

After 50 minutes, the top of the loaf should be darkly colored. The sides and bottom should not be as dark as the top.

Remove the pan with oven mitts or thick kitchen towels and carefully tilt it to turn the loaf out. If a hard rap on the counter doesn't free the loaf, use a folded kitchen towel to firmly grab one edge of the pan with one hand and use your other hand to pry the loaf out. (Use more cooking spray next time.) Let the loaf cool on a rack, so air can circulate around it, for at least 30 minutes before slicing; 1 hour is better.

How to Convert Same-Day Recipes to Overnight Cold-Proof Recipes

The Standard #2 overnight version is a good example of how to take a Same-Day recipe and convert it to one that has you proof the shaped loaf in the refrigerator overnight and then bake it in the morning. The flour blends are the same, and you will get near equivalent results. The adjustments are simple:

- Start the recipe later in the day. If you begin at 6 p.m., the loaf will be ready to bake between 7:30 a.m. and 9:30 a.m.

- Decrease the water in the dough by 10 grams / 2 teaspoons (2 percent of the flour weight) and keep all the other ingredient quantities the same.

- Shorten the first rise time by about 30 minutes, and consider it done when the dough has reached about ½ inch, rather than ¼ inch, below the 2-quart line on a dough tub with volume markings.

- Shape it the same way and then use your hand to apply a light film of water on the top of the loaf after you've put it into the pan to prevent the dough from sticking to the proofing bag as it expands in the refrigerator overnight. Lightly punch down the dough to de-gas it a bit if you put it into a bread pan. This is not necessary if you have it in a proofing basket for Dutch-oven baking in the morning. Then place your pan or basket in a nonperforated plastic bag, but do not make it tight at the top (you could cover the loaf loosely with plastic wrap). Leave plenty of room for the dough to expand, a few inches, and tuck the bag under the pan. The bag will peel off the dough easily in the morning if you applied the film of water.

- Bake the same way. About 45 minutes prior to baking, preheat the oven to 450°F / 230°C. Place the bread on the center of the middle oven rack. Turn down the heat to 425°F / 220°C and bake for about 50 minutes.

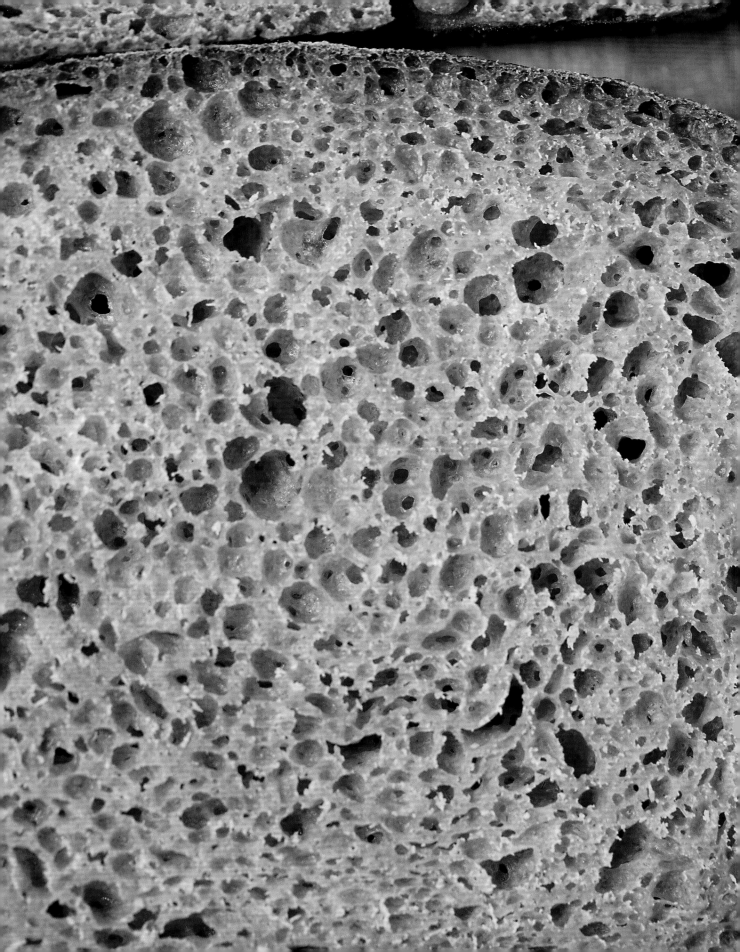

100% SPELT PAN BREAD

Open pan, lidded pan, or Dutch oven

This recipe could work with many stone-milled whole-grain wheat flours. Spelt is considered the third of the three ancient wheat varieties, though it is younger than both emmer and einkorn. It also has more gluten than emmer or einkorn, and while flour from those two varieties bake flavorful brick breads, the rise from spelt gives this loaf a lighter-textured, dark brown crumb. Other heirloom wheat varieties, such as Red Fife and Rouge de Bordeaux (both widely grown in the United States and in France in the 1800s), or comparatively recent high-quality crossbreeds, like Edison, would work beautifully with this recipe or in any of the 50 percent whole-grain recipes in this book. Durum wheat is another option—it is stronger than other wheats, is delicious, and is the only wheat flour with a golden yellow color. If you use durum, you should add another 30 to 40 grams of water in the recipe.

Stone milling brings out the best in these wheat varieties, as the process literally crushes the wheat berries and all their contents. The germ of the wheat berry contains oils that flavor the flour, and the bran is a good source of dietary fiber. These 100 percent whole-grain breads don't rise too much above the bread pan, so don't be disappointed by that—it's the way they are. The interior of the fully baked loaf has plenty of small holes, and what these loaves lack in volume, they more than make up for it in great flavor. This bread will keep for up to 6 days.

THIS RECIPE MAKES 1 PAN LOAF OF A LITTLE MORE THAN 2 POUNDS.

First rise
About 3 hours at 70°F / 21°C room temperature.
Faster if warmer, slower if cooler.

Proof time
10 to 14 hours in the refrigerator.

Bake
Preheat to 450°F / 230°C for 45 minutes,
bake at 425°F / 220°C for about 50 minutes.

Sample schedule
Begin at 6 p.m., finish mixing at 6:30 p.m., shape into a loaf at 9:30 p.m.,
and bake at 9 a.m. the next day.

Ingredient	Quantity	Baker's Percentage
Whole-spelt flour	500 g / 3½ cups + 1 Tbsp + ½ tsp	100%
Water (90° to 95°F / 32° to 35°C)	425 g / 1¾ cups + 1 tsp	85%
Fine sea salt	11 g / 2¼ tsp	2.2%
Instant dried yeast	3 g / 1 tsp	0.6%
Levain (optional)	100 g / ½ cup	9% of total flour (if used)

1. Autolyse

Measure 425 grams (90° to 95°F / 32° to 35°C) water into a 6-quart round tub or similar container. If you have a levain, add 100 grams from the refrigerator—you can weigh it directly into the dough tub with its water. Stir a bit with your fingers to loosen up the culture. Add 500 grams whole-spelt flour. Mix it by hand until all is incorporated.

Sprinkle 11 grams fine sea salt evenly across the top of the autolyse dough. Then sprinkle 3 grams instant dried yeast on top of that. Let them rest there, where they will partially dissolve.

Cover and let rest for 30 minutes. (I let whole-grain, high-hydration dough rest at this stage longer than white-flour dough.)

2. Mix

Mix by hand, wetting your working hand before mixing so the dough doesn't stick to you. Reach underneath the dough and grab about one-fourth of it. Gently stretch this section and fold it over the top to the other side of the dough. Repeat three more times with the remaining dough until the salt and yeast are fully enclosed.

Use the pincer method to fully integrate the ingredients. Make five or six pincer cuts across the entire mass of dough. Then fold the dough over itself a few times. Repeat, alternately cutting and folding, until all the ingredients are fully integrated. Let the dough rest for a few minutes, then fold for another 30 seconds or until the dough tightens up. The whole process should take about 5 minutes. The target dough temperature at the end of the mix is about 75°F / 24°C. Cover the tub and let the dough rise until the next fold.

3. Fold & First Rise

This dough needs two folds (see page 41). Apply the folds during the first hour after mixing the dough. Apply the first fold about 10 minutes after mixing and the second when you see the dough spread out in the tub. If need be, it's okay to fold later; just be sure to leave it alone for the last hour of rising.

When the dough is about two and a half times its original volume, about 3 hours after the mix, it's ready to be made up into a loaf and put into its pan. If you are using a 6-quart dough tub, the ideal point is when the edge of the dough has reached about 1/2 inch below the 2-quart line on the side of the tub, and the dough will be domed—not flattened, not collapsed. If it reaches the 2-quart line on your dough tub, you have caught it a little late, but you can lightly punch down the dough to de-gas it before shaping it into a loaf. If the room is cool and the dough is taking longer, let it continue to rise until it reaches this amount of volume expansion. If you're not using a marked dough tub, you'll have to eyeball it. Use your best judgment.

4. Remove the Dough from Its Tub

Moderately flour a work surface about 12 inches wide. Flour your hands and sprinkle a bit of flour around the edges of the tub. Tip the tub slightly and gently work your floured free hand beneath the dough to loosen it from the bottom of the tub. Then turn the tub on its side and ease the dough out onto the work surface without pulling or tearing it.

Even if your bread pan is nonstick, you might want to give it a light spritz of cooking spray. Nonstick pans are sometimes not 100 percent nonstick if they have been used a lot.

5. Shape

With floured hands, pick up the dough and ease it back onto the work surface in a somewhat even, rectangular shape. You will stretch and fold this slack dough into something equal to the width of your bread pan.

Following the shaping instructions on pages 43 to 44, with two floured hands, stretch the dough, simultaneously pulling it right and left (just spread your hands both ways at the same time to stretch out the dough) until it resists—two to three times its original width—and then fold the ends back over each other, creating a "packet" the width of your baking pan.

Brush off any loose flour from the top of the dough and do a roll-up motion from the bottom up or from top to bottom to form a tube of dough that's about the same width as your baking pan. Place the dough seam-up into the pan. The seam is usually visible; it's the part of the rolled-up dough where the outer edges have joined to enclose the interior parts of the newly shaped loaf.

6. Proof

Use your hand to apply a light film of water across the entire top surface of the dough after it's in its pan. This prevents the dough from sticking to the plastic bag as it expands in the refrigerator overnight. Lightly punch down the dough to de-gas it a bit. Then place your bread pan in a nonperforated plastic bag, but do not make it too tight at the top. Leave plenty of room for the dough to expand, a few inches, and tuck the bag under the pan. Put the pan into the refrigerator.

The next morning, the dough should have inflated up to the pan line if you are using the USA Pan that measures 8½ by 4½ by 2¾ inches. See photos of perfect proofing on page 50.

7. Preheat

About 45 minutes prior to baking, position a rack in the middle of the oven and preheat the oven to 450°F / 230°C.

8. Bake

Remove the pan from the plastic bag and place it on the center of the oven rack. Turn down the heat to 425°F / 220°C and bake. After 30 minutes, check for even baking (give the pan a turn if the baking is uneven) and bake for another 20 minutes. Because this dough has more water than traditional pan loaves, it needs a longer time than you might think to bake the inside fully and to color the sides and give them enough strength to avoid post-bake collapse.

After 50 minutes, the top of the loaf should be darkly colored. The sides and bottom will not be as dark as the top.

Remove the pan with oven mitts or thick kitchen towels and carefully tilt it to turn the loaf out. If a hard rap on the counter doesn't free the loaf, use a folded kitchen towel to firmly grab one edge of the pan with one hand and use your other hand to pry the loaf out. (Use more cooking spray next time.) Let the loaf cool on a rack, so air can circulate around it, for at least 30 minutes before slicing; 1 hour is better.

NEW YORK–STYLE RYE BREAD WITH CARAWAY

Open pan, lidded pan, or Dutch oven

If you say "rye bread" to many Americans, this loaf is what will likely be in their memory banks. *Jewish rye* and *deli rye* are other names for bread very similar to what this recipe makes. This bread has a strong association with Jewish delicatessens; in New York, many of them buy from bakeries that make their rye bread with a sourdough starter. This version is a hybrid, using store-bought yeast and an optional—but recommended—100 grams of this book's levain.

This is the bread you want for a classic Reuben or pastrami sandwich. A tuna melt or grilled cheese sandwich would be good on this too. I'd enjoy it as a patty-melt bread, or as a trencher underneath a serving of braised meat with its broth—for example, braised pork shoulder with sauerkraut.

This recipe uses an overnight cold proof after the loaf is made up in the evening. You bake it first thing in the morning. If you want to convert this recipe to a same-day mix-and-bake loaf—6 hours from beginning to out of the oven—extend the first rise to about 3½ hours and, after making up the loaf and putting it into the bread pan, let it proof for about an hour, until the dough rises a little bit above the pan rim, then bake.

THIS RECIPE MAKES 1 PAN LOAF OF ABOUT 2 POUNDS.

First rise
About 3 hours at 70°F / 21°C room temperature.
Faster if warmer, slower if cooler.

Proof time
10 to 11 hours in the refrigerator.

Bake
Preheat to 450°F / 230°C for 45 minutes,
bake at 425°F / 220°C for about 50 minutes.

Sample schedule
Begin at 6 p.m., finish mixing at 6:30 p.m., shape into a loaf at 9:30 p.m.,
and bake at 8 a.m. the next day. (Rye's weaker gluten doesn't hold as long,
so aim for a little shorter cold proof time than the other breads.)

Ingredient	Quantity	Baker's Percentage
White bread flour	400 g / 2¾ cups + 2 tsp	80%
Light or dark rye flour	100 g / ¾ cup + 1 tsp	20%
Water (90° to 95°F / 32° to 35°C)	370 g / 1½ cups + 2 tsp	74%
Fine sea salt	11 g / 2¼ tsp	2.2%
Caraway seeds	12 g / 2 Tbsp + 2 tsp	2.4%
Instant dried yeast	3 g / 1 tsp	0.6%
Levain (optional)	100 g / ½ cup	9% of total flour (if used)

1. Autolyse

Measure 400 grams white bread flour, 100 grams rye flour, and 12 grams caraway seeds into a container, then blend them by hand. Measure 370 grams (90° to 95°F / 32° to 35°C) water into a 6-quart round tub or similar container. If you have a levain, add 100 grams from the refrigerator. Stir a bit with your fingers to loosen up the culture. Add the blended flour-seed mix. Mix it by hand until all is incorporated.

Sprinkle 11 grams fine sea salt evenly across the top of the autolyse dough. Then sprinkle 3 grams instant dried yeast on top of that. Let them rest there, where they will partially dissolve.

Cover and let rest for 20 to 30 minutes.

2. Mix

Mix by hand, wetting your working hand before mixing so the dough doesn't stick to you. Reach underneath the dough and grab about one-fourth of it. Gently stretch this section and fold it over the top to the other side of the dough. Repeat three more times with the remaining dough until the salt and yeast are fully enclosed. (You'll notice the rye dough doesn't stretch as much as the doughs made with just wheat flour.)

Use the pincer method to fully integrate the ingredients. Make five or six pincer cuts across the entire mass of dough. Then fold the dough over itself a few times. Repeat, alternately cutting and folding, until all the ingredients are fully integrated. Let the dough rest for a few minutes, then fold for another 30 seconds or until the dough tightens up. The whole process should take about 5 minutes. The target dough temperature at the end of the mix is 75°F / 24°C. Cover the tub and let the dough rise until the next fold.

3. Fold & First Rise

Rye dough sticks to the bottom of the dough tub. This task is easier if you have a small, plastic dough scraper to scoop under the dough to help you fold it; but if you don't, just use your hand. This dough needs two folds (see page 41). It's easiest to apply the folds during the first hour after mixing the dough. Apply the first fold about 10 minutes after mixing and the second when you see the dough spread out in the tub.

When the dough is about two and a half times its original volume, about 3 hours after the mix, it is ready to be made up into a loaf and put into its pan. If you are using a 6-quart dough tub, the ideal point is when the edge of the dough has reached about ½ inch below the 2-quart line on the side of the tub, and the dough will be domed—not flattened, not collapsed. If it reaches the 2-quart line on your dough tub, you have caught it a little late, but you can lightly punch down the dough to de-gas it before shaping it into a loaf. If the room is cool and the dough is taking longer, let it continue to rise until it reaches this ideal amount of volume expansion. If you're not using a marked dough tub, you'll have to eyeball it. Use your best judgment.

4. Remove the Dough from Its Tub

Moderately flour a work surface about 12 inches wide. Flour your hands and sprinkle a bit of flour around the edges of the tub. Tip the tub slightly and gently work your floured free hand or the flexible dough scraper beneath the dough to loosen it from the bottom of the tub. Then turn the tub on its side and ease the dough out onto the work surface without pulling or tearing it.

Even if your bread pan is nonstick, you might want to give it a light spritz of cooking spray. Nonstick pans are sometimes not 100 percent nonstick if they have been used a lot.

5. Shape

With floured hands, pick up the dough and ease it back onto the work surface in a somewhat even, rectangular shape. You will stretch and fold this slack dough into something equal to the width of your bread pan.

Following the shaping instructions on pages 43 to 44 with two floured hands, stretch the dough, simultaneously pulling it right and left (just spread your hands both ways at the same time to stretch out the dough) until it resists—two to three times its original width—and then fold the ends back over each other, creating a "packet" the width of your baking pan.

Brush off any loose flour from the top of the dough and do a roll-up motion from the bottom up or from top to bottom to form a tube of dough that's about the same width as your baking pan. Place the dough seam-up into the pan. The seam is usually visible; it's the part of the rolled-up dough where the outer edges have joined to enclose the interior parts of the newly shaped loaf.

6. Proof

Use your hand to apply a light film of water across the entire top surface of the dough after it's in its pan. This prevents the dough from sticking to the plastic bag as it expands in the refrigerator overnight. Lightly punch down the dough to de-gas it a bit. Then place your bread pan in a nonperforated plastic bag, but don't make it too tight at the top. Leave plenty of room for the dough to expand, a few inches, and tuck the bag under the pan. Put the pan into the refrigerator.

The next morning, the dough should have inflated above the pan line if you are using the USA Pan that measures 8½ by 4½ by 2¾ inches. It might look like too much! No fear. A little bit of droop over the edges is desirable, and it should look domed in the middle. In a larger bread pan, it is less likely the dough will rise above the pan line. See photos of perfect proofing on page 50.

7. Preheat

About 45 minutes prior to baking, position a rack in the middle of the oven and preheat the oven to 450°F / 230°C.

8. Bake

Remove the pan from the plastic bag and place it in the center of the oven rack. Turn down the heat to 425°F / 220°C and bake. After 30 minutes, check for even baking (give the pan a turn if the baking is uneven) and bake for another 20 minutes. It needs a longer time than you might think to bake the inside fully and to color the sides and give them enough strength to avoid post-bake collapse.

After 50 minutes, the top of the loaf should be darkly colored. The sides and bottom should not be as dark as the top.

Remove the pan with oven mitts or thick kitchen towels and carefully tilt it to turn the loaf out. If a hard rap on the counter doesn't free the loaf, use a folded kitchen towel to firmly grab one edge of the pan with one hand and use your other hand to pry the loaf out. (Use more cooking spray next time.) Let the loaf cool on a rack, so air can circulate around it, for at least 30 minutes before slicing; 1 hour is better.

CHAPTER 6
ENRICHED-DOUGH RECIPES

There is a world of pan breads, called enriched breads, that include milk, butter, sugar, and eggs. When made well, they have a radiant goodness. You may not have considered these to be within your realm. Yet they are. The two recipes that follow are not as complicated as you may think, and they have taste and texture that you might have thought could only come from a very good bakery. These enriched breads have a wide range of uses and freeze well. Each can be baked in a lidded pan to get a uniform, squared-edge shape, or they can be made into balls that fit in the pan next to one another and bake into a cool-looking loaf of three beautiful, bulging rounds. Brioche is a classic, requiring a very specific dough-mixing process to get a good rise and a high-quality crumb. I'll work you through my trials and errors, hopefully with instructions that you find workable and repeatable. Shokupan, or Japanese Milk Bread, is delightful. Prior to making the dough, you cook a flour-water paste on the stove. This goes into the dough after it cools, and it gives the bread a pull-apart texture that is unique and super-satisfying. It makes a wonderful sandwich bread too.

Both of these recipes require a stand mixer and are a slight departure from the standard eight steps.

Professional Tips on Using Your Stand Mixer

I don't know how the dough was mixed in Marie Antoinette's day, but I can't imagine integrating this amount of butter into the dough without a good mechanical mixer. From a professional baker's point of view, a home stand mixer, such as a KitchenAid, requires a chin-scratching learning curve. KitchenAid may be the most popular mixer brand in American kitchens, but its C-shaped dough hook doesn't integrate and mix a variety of doughs as well as its whip and paddle attachments whip and mix.

After a few attempts, I did manage to get this dough to where it mixes well enough to incorporate the dry ingredients, develop the gluten, and then blend in the butter. "How do I make it work like my Hobart mixer or my bread dough mixer at my bakery?" was a continuous question for a few days, but it's doable! This dough comes out looking just like my bakery's brioche dough. It has the right satiny sheen and an elastic stretch to it.

For best results, be sure to have the dough moist enough to fully integrate all the ingredients and not leave strings and pebbles of flour in the bottom of the mixer bowl. Follow my measurements precisely. This recipe holds back some of the flour at the initial mix to let the dough form and then adds the rest of the flour and it incorporates just fine. If you don't do that, you'll likely get threads of dry flour in the bottom of the mixer bowl just spinning around and around. (This can be fixed by removing the dough, hand kneading in the dry ingredients, and then returning the dough to the mixer bowl for the next step.)

Another issue is that sometimes the dough climbs up the dough hook. If the dough climbs too high in your mixer, it could creep up to the gears, or, with larger batches, the hook sometimes pushes the dough out of the bowl. You want to stay with the mixer while it's working to keep an eye on it and to get used to how it works. This is good anyway, as you need to monitor to make sure the dough hook is actually doing something and not just moving a ball of dough around and around with nothing happening. I worked through this to make sure the dough size and hydration work on my KitchenAid Pro 4½-quart mixer. Every couple of minutes, I'd scrape down the sides of the bowl, peel the dough off the hook, reposition it, and loosen the dough that sticks to the middle of the bottom of the bowl. Then I'd resume mixing.

Your mixer may be a different brand or size than mine. If you don't feel your mixer is doing its job, it's okay if, before adding the butter, you remove the dough from the mixer once or twice and hand knead it on a floured surface. You need good development of the gluten in the dough before the addition of butter. If all your mixer does is spin the dough around the bowl without the dough hook going through it, you will need to knead the dough by hand for a bit. When incorporating the butter, let the machine do all the work.

BRIOCHE

Lidded pan or open pan (for shaped rounds)

This recipe requires a stand mixer with a 4- to 5-quart mixing bowl and a dough hook

Fresh, warm brioche is like a Hawaiian sunset on a winter day: no matter what else is going on, you are about to have a wonderful moment. As the bread bakes, your nose gets the first tease when aromatic fingers of warm brioche air glide by to tempt you with a promise of what's to come. Good brioche dissolves when you chew it and leaves behind buttery fermented dough flavors that linger like a pleasant, uninterrupted daydream. Slice it thickly, or go traditional and pull it apart and eat it with your hands. It's just . . . great.

With a good brioche dough, you can make a squared-edge rectangular loaf for slicing, a pull-apart loaf of multiple dough rounds that rise and bake together, or the classic French knobby brioche à tête baked in a fluted pan. I have two ways of making brioche with this dough recipe: one for a lidded pan and one made up of three rounded-lobes that rise together above the pan height.

There is no water in a good brioche dough. The hydration comes mostly from eggs and a little bit of milk. Then, once the dough is mixed, you add butter. Lots of butter—40 to 60 percent of the flour weight is a typical amount of butter for a brioche dough.

One warning that I need to put up front with this recipe: It is possible to put too much dough into a lidded dough pan, my preferred vessel for this loaf. If you do, as the dough rises in the oven, it will burst out of the lidded pan and the excess can drain onto the floor of the oven. When that happens, with so much egg and butter in the dough, it's going to smoke. A lot. Please be careful and stay with your oven for the first 15 to 20 minutes of your bake to make sure this doesn't happen to you. The lidded-pan recipe is calculated to match the capacity of the CHEFMADE lidded pan (8.4 by 4.8 by 4.5 inches) that I recommend in the equipment section of this book. I had to pick one. This problem is only a lidded-pan problem. If you bake the open-pan loaf, the risen dough will stay intact as it rises above the rim of the pan.

THIS RECIPE MAKES 1 PAN LOAF OF ABOUT 2 POUNDS.

First rise
About 3 hours at 70°F / 21°C room temperature.
Faster if warmer, slower if cooler.

Proof time
About 2 hours at 70°F / 21°C room temperature.

Bake
Preheat to 375°F / 190°C for 45 minutes,
bake at 375°F / 190°C for about 40 minutes.

Sample schedule
Begin at 9:30 a.m., finish mixing at 10 a.m., shape into a loaf at 1 p.m.,
and bake at 3 p.m.

Weigh the ingredients separately before starting, then you can focus on
mixing without distraction. Once the dough has completed its first rise, the
directions become specific to each type of loaf: open pan or lidded pan.

Ingredient	Quantity	Baker's Percentage
White bread flour	330 g / 2⅓ cups + 1¼ tsp	100%
Egg	200 g (4 large eggs)	60%
Milk (cold)	33 g / 2 Tbsp + ¾ tsp	10%
Granulated sugar	40 g / 2 Tbsp + 1¼ tsp	12%
Fine sea salt	7 g / scant 1½ tsp	2%
Instant dried yeast	6 g / 2 tsp	1.8%
Levain (optional)	50 g / ¼ cup	7.6% of total flour (if used)
Unsalted butter (cold)	165 g / ¾ cup	50%

1a. Mix, Stage 1

In this order and without stirring, put into the mixer bowl 4 eggs, 33 grams milk, 6 grams yeast, and, if you have a levain, 50 grams from the refrigerator. Let rest for 1 to 2 minutes, then add 280 grams of the flour (all but 50 grams of the total) and then mix with the dough hook on the lowest speed until all the flour is incorporated. Add the remaining 50 grams flour and mix for 5 minutes on medium-low speed (the second speed on my KitchenAid). Scrape down the sides of the bowl with a spatula or rounded-edge dough scraper and add the scraped-dough schmutz to the dough.

1b. Mix, Stage 2

Add 40 grams sugar and 7 grams salt to the bowl and mix on medium-low speed for 5 minutes. Stop the mix once or twice to scrape down the sides of the bowl and pull the dough off the hook to give it a fresh start. Then resume the mix, making sure the dough has spent 3 minutes mixing on medium-low speed as a cohesive mass. You need to develop the gluten in the dough via mixing before adding in the butter. If the mixer looks like it is just pushing the ball of dough around the mixer but nothing is really happening, stop the mixer, remove the dough from the bowl, and hand knead it for a couple minutes on a floured surface, then return the dough to the mixer bowl for the butter step.

1c. Mix, Stage 3

Cut 165 grams cold butter into about twenty-five small pieces. Set a timer for 10 minutes; this is the total time to mix in the butter. Add two-thirds of the butter to the dough and cover with 8 to 10 grams

(about 1 tablespoon) white bread flour to give the butter some grip and aid the integration into the dough; mix on medium-low speed for a couple minutes. Then add the rest of the butter and mix for the remainder of the 10 minutes.

At the end of the Stage 3 mix, the butter should be fully incorporated into the dough with no visible pieces. The dough should have a satiny sheen and be very smooth. It should be stretchy when you remove it from the bowl. (I like to use a flexible pastry scraper to help me remove the dough from the bowl.)

At the beginning of the mix, the dough starts out cold. The friction from the mix process raises the temperature, and my average dough temperature at the end of the mix is about 72°F / 22°C.

2. Remove from the Mixer Bowl & First Rise

Lightly flour a work surface about 12 inches wide. Flour your hands and remove the dough from the mixer bowl, lifting it up from the bottom (use a flexible scraper to help release the dough if it is stuck to the bottom of the bowl), and place on the floured work surface. Stretch and fold the dough over itself several times and round it to form a tight ball. Dip the bottom (seam side) in a little bit of flour and place seam down into a dough tub with a lid or into a large bowl and cover airtight to rise at room temperature until doubled in size, about 3 hours.

Even if your bread pan is nonstick, you might want to give it a light spritz of cooking spray. Nonstick pans are sometimes not 100 percent nonstick if they have been used a lot.

3. Shape

You will stretch and fold this stretchy, slack dough into something equal to the width of your bread pan. With floured hands, pick up the dough and ease it back onto the work surface in a somewhat even, rectangular shape.

LIDDED-PAN LOAF

Following the shaping instructions on pages 43 to 44, with two floured hands, stretch the dough, simultaneously pulling it right and left (just spread your hands both ways at the same time to stretch out the dough) until it resists—at least three times its original width—and then fold the ends back over each other, creating a "packet" the width of your baking pan.

Brush off any loose flour from the top of the dough and do a roll-up motion from the bottom up or from top to bottom to form a tube of dough that's about the same width as your baking pan. Place the dough seam up or down into the pan; either way is fine. Put the lid on the pan.

OPEN-PAN LOAF

Using a dough cutter, cut the dough into three equal pieces, each weighing about 250 grams (or about 265 grams if you used the levain). The math is not precise because some dough will have stuck to the tub or bowl.

Preshape in rounds using the stretch-and-fold technique. For each piece of dough, grab quarter segments of the dough, one at a time, and stretch out, then fold them back over the dough piece, until you have created a round. Then tighten the dough into a ball on a clean unfloured surface so the bottom half will have some grip to aid the tightening.

Pull each ball, seam down, toward you, with a downward motion against the surface to tighten. Turn and repeat. Cover and let rest for 10 minutes, then repeat for each ball.

Place the balls, seam down and side by side, in the pan. Cover with plastic wrap.

4. Proof

The timing is important here, and the visual cues are a little different for the two styles of brioche loaves.

Lidded Pan: When the dough has risen just shy (about 1/4 inch) of the lid, it's ready to bake. If it's touching the lid, that's fine too.

Open Pan: When the dough is pressing into the plastic covering it, it's ready to bake. The plastic should peel right off thanks to the buttery dough.

Plan on baking the loaf about 2 hours after it is shaped, assuming a room temperature of about 70°F / 21°C. If your kitchen is warmer, it will be optimally proofed earlier.

5. Preheat

About 45 minutes prior to baking, position a rack in the middle of the oven and preheat the oven to 375°F / 190°C.

6. Bake

If using an open pan, peel off the plastic wrap. Place the lidded or open pan on the center of the oven rack. Bake for 30 minutes, then check the open pan for even baking (give it a turn if the baking is uneven) and bake for about 10 minutes more. The lidded-pan loaf can finish baking, lid on the whole time, for the full 40 minutes without any intervention.

The open-pan loaf tends to bake pretty dark on top, but it needs to finish so the sides have enough structure to prevent a post-bake inward collapse; so don't take it out too early. If the top of your brioche is coloring too fast, create a tent with aluminum foil and lightly cover the loaf about 30 minutes into the bake. (In my oven, it baked fine without covering.)

Remove the pan with oven mitts or thick kitchen towels and immediately and carefully tilt it to turn the loaf out. (If you do not remove brioche from its baking pan immediately, the sides and bottom will steam and collapse inward.) Let the loaf cool on a rack, so air can circulate around it, for at least 30 minutes before slicing; 1 hour is better.

SHOKUPAN, OR JAPANESE MILK BREAD

Lidded pan or open pan
(for shaped rounds)

This recipe requires a
stand mixer with a 4- to
5-quart mixing bowl and
a dough hook

First, you notice the springy texture of a thick slice of this enticing bread. Then, you discover the delight of its slightly sweet, milky flavor. It's somehow different from other enriched white breads, like French pain de mie. Japanese milk bread, also known as shokupan, is made from an enriched dough that's more milk than butter. But its defining nature comes from cooking a small amount of flour and water into a water roux that is later added to the dough. It takes about 3 minutes in a saucepan on the stove top, stirring the entire time. Called *yudane*, the water roux cooks into a gluey paste, and the first time you do it, you have to wonder what exactly is up with this? In technical terms, you have pre-gelatinized some of the starch, allowing it to hold a lot more water, and that in turn changes everything about the texture of this bread. It's kind of crazy the way it works.

When mixing 4 to 5 parts water (recipes vary) to 1 part flour, you would expect a very thin slurry. But after the roux is cooked and cooled, it has a texture like silicone gel. It doesn't let much of that water go to hydrate the rest of the dough when it all gets mixed together, so by the numbers you would expect a different, slack dough texture, when, in fact, it mixes to what feels like an old-fashioned bread dough. The roux's gelatinized starch in the dough also holds on to its water while the bread bakes, and you get a soft and springy bread that takes a long time to stale. Super-cool.

In this recipe, milk bread is baked in a lidded pan so the slices will be uniformly sized with squared-off edges. It can also be adapted to an open pan, like the other pan loaves in this book, or, like brioche, shaped into three balls of dough that rise and bake together in one pan to form pull-apart pieces. (If you want to go that route, follow the Brioche instructions for making an open-pan loaf on page 172. You can divide this dough into three pieces of about 290 grams each.)

If you'd like to make Japanese convenience-store-style sandwiches, this is the bread you want. Konbini egg salad with the cute half-egg in the middle? Instagrammable sandwich pictures are your thing? Here you go.

Try making a steak sandwich with toasted slices of shokupan, you'll go nuts. Pizza toast is made from this bread at some retro Japanese cafés and kissaten (coffee shops). The bread is thickly sliced and then topped with just sauce and cheese or more fancifully, depending on the whim of the shop. Crust, no crust, or even partial-crust cuts become a signature in the world of Japanese pizza toast.

The roux must be cooked to a specific temperature range, 150° to 175°F / 66° to 79°C. Some references identify 149°F / 65°C as the perfect temperature; others say 175°F / 79°C. I had similar results throughout this range in multiple tests. Cooking the roux too hot will break it down from what you need to achieve the correct textural effect in the bread. In my tests, I preheated a small saucepan over medium heat, then added the water and flour, turned down the heat to medium-low, and cooked the roux for about 3 minutes, stirring constantly (a large soupspoon worked a lot better for me than a whisk and made measuring the temperature easier because the whisk holds so much goop in its wires). The roux forms a paste with a texture that I can only describe as like glue and then solidifies into a soft gel. If you don't have a probe thermometer to measure the roux temperature, follow my 3-minute cooking process. If you cook the roux in a large pan, however, it might be ready in just 1 minute.

As with the Brioche recipe, this dough is sized to match the capacity of the CHEFMADE lidded pan (8.4 by 4.8 by 4.5-inches) that I recommend on page 28.

THIS RECIPE MAKES 1 PAN LOAF OF ABOUT 2 POUNDS.

First rise
About 2 hours at 70°F / 21°C room temperature.
Faster if warmer, slower if cooler.

Proof time
About 1½ hours at 70°F / 21°C room temperature.

Bake
Preheat to 375°F / 190°C for 45 minutes,
bake at 375°F / 190°C for about 45 minutes.

Sample schedule
Begin at 9:30 a.m., finish mixing at 10 a.m.,
shape into a loaf at noon, and bake at 1:45 p.m.

Weigh the ingredients separately before starting,
then you can focus on mixing without distraction.

WATER ROUX

Ingredient	Quantity	Baker's Percentage
Water	125 g / ¼ cup + 2 Tbsp + 2 tsp	29.4%
White bread flour	25 g / 2 Tbsp + 2¾ tsp	6%

FINAL DOUGH

Ingredient	Quantity	Baker's Percentage
White bread flour*	400 g / 2¾ cups + 2 tsp	94%
Whole milk (cold)	215 g / 1 cup + 2 tsp	50.6%
Granulated sugar	30 g / 2 Tbsp + 1¼ tsp	7.5%
Fine sea salt	8 g / 1½ tsp	1.9%
Instant dried yeast	8 g / 2¾ tsp	1.9%
Unsalted butter (cold)	60 g / ¼ cup + 1 tsp	14%
Water roux	150 g	water = 29.4% flour = 6%

* Total flour includes the flour in the roux (100% Baker's Percentage) = 425 grams.

1. Cook the Roux

Preheat a small saucepan over medium heat for about 1 minute. Measure 125 grams water into the pan and add 25 grams flour. Cook over medium to medium-low heat, stirring constantly with a large soupspoon, for about 3 minutes. It will start out thin but end up a mashed potato–like gluey paste. It's done when the temperature registers between 150° and 175°F / 66° and 79°C. Let the roux cool for 10 minutes or more off the heat.

2. Scale Your Ingredients

While the roux is resting, measure out into separate bowls 400 grams flour, 215 grams cold whole milk, 30 grams sugar, 8 grams fine sea salt, 8 grams instant dried yeast, and 60 grams cold butter.

3a. Mix, Stage 1

Pour 215 grams milk into the mixer bowl and sprinkle 8 grams instant dried yeast on top. Let rest for 1 to 2 minutes; you do not need to stir. Add 400 grams flour to the milk and yeast in the bowl, then add the roux (be sure it's cooler than 110°F / 43°C). Mix with the dough hook on the lowest speed until all the flour is incorporated, then continue mixing for another 3 minutes. The dough should come together in a ball.

3b. Mix, Stage 2

Add 30 grams sugar and 8 grams fine sea salt to the dough and mix on the lowest speed for 5 minutes. (This process worked without much manipulation of the dough in my mixer.) If you need to scrape down the sides and bottom of your mixer bowl, or remove the dough from the dough hook once or twice, please do so. The goal is to incorporate all the ingredients and develop the gluten before adding cold butter at the end.

3c. Mix, Stage 3

Cut the cold butter into about a dozen pieces, add to the dough, and mix on medium-low speed (the second speed on my KitchenAid) until the pieces are no longer visible, about 5 minutes.

At the beginning of the mix, the dough starts out cold. The friction from the mix process raises the temperature, and my average dough temperature at the end of the mix is about 72°F / 22°C.

4. Remove from the Mixer Bowl & First Rise

Lightly flour a work surface about 12 inches wide. Flour your hands and remove the dough from the mixer bowl, lifting it up from the bottom (use a flexible scraper to help release the dough if it is stuck to the bottom of the bowl), and place on the floured work surface. Stretch and fold the dough over itself several times and round it to form a tight ball. Dip the bottom (seam side) in a little bit of flour and place seam down into a dough tub with a lid or into a large bowl and cover airtight to rise at room temperature until doubled in size, about 2 hours.

Even if your bread pan is nonstick, you might want to give it a light spritz of cooking spray. Nonstick pans are sometimes not 100 percent nonstick if they have been used a lot.

5. Shape

You will stretch and fold this dough into something equal to the width of your bread pan. With floured hands, pick up the dough and ease it back onto the work surface in a somewhat even, rectangular shape.

Following the shaping instructions on pages 43 to 44, with two floured hands, stretch the dough, simultaneously pulling it right and left (just spread your hands both ways at the same time to stretch out the dough) until it resists—two to three times its original width—and then fold the ends back over each other, creating a "packet" the width of your baking pan.

Brush off any loose flour from the top of the dough and do a roll-up motion from the bottom up or from top to bottom to form a tube of dough that's about the same width as your baking pan. Place the dough seam up or down into the pan; either way is fine. Put the lid on the pan and let it sit out at room temperature.

6. Proof

When the dough has risen to just shy (about ¼ inch) of the lid, it's ready to bake. If it's touching the lid, that's okay too.

Plan on baking the loaf about 1½ hours after it is shaped, assuming a room temperature of about 70°F / 21°C. If your kitchen is warmer, it will be optimally proofed earlier.

7. Preheat

About 45 minutes prior to baking, position a rack in the middle of the oven and preheat the oven to 375°F / 190°C.

8. Bake

Place the pan on the center of the oven rack and bake for about 40 minutes, lid on the whole time. Check for color about 35 minutes into it and then finish so the sides have enough structure to prevent a post-bake inward collapse.

Remove the pan with oven mitts or thick kitchen towels and immediately and carefully tilt it to turn the loaf out. (If you do not remove the milk bread from its baking pan immediately, the sides and bottom will steam and collapse inward.) Let the loaf cool on a rack, so air can circulate around it, for at least 30 minutes before slicing; 1 hour is better.

EGG SALAD, KONBINI-STYLE

The key elements in this recipe are using an additional egg yolk in the mixture, the rice vinegar, and Kewpie mayonnaise (which is easy to order online). This variation is from Yuki Nishitani, a former baker at Trifecta Tavern & Bakery and Ken's Artisan Bakery.

THIS RECIPE MAKES 6 MINI EGG-SALAD SANDWICHES.

Ingredients	Quantity
Egg	5 large eggs
Ice cubes (for ice bath)	
Kewpie mayonnaise	5 Tbsp
Rice vinegar	1 tsp
Granulated sugar	1 tsp, or to taste
Salt and pepper	
Shokupan Bread	4 slices
Softened unsalted butter (for smearing)	

Fill a 2-quart or larger saucepan with water and bring to a boil over high heat. Add the eggs straight from the refrigerator and boil for 10 minutes. While the eggs are boiling, fill a medium bowl with ice cubes and cold water. When the eggs are ready, immediately transfer them to the ice bath, immersing them in the ice-cold water for 1 to 2 minutes.

Peel the eggs. Remove the white from one of the eggs and reserve for another use. On a cutting board, chop the four whole eggs and additional yolk into medium-small pieces. Transfer to a medium bowl; add the mayonnaise, vinegar, and sugar; and season with salt and pepper. Gently combine with a rubber spatula until all the ingredients are evenly blended. Taste and adjust with more sugar, salt, and pepper if needed.

Cut the crusts off the bread slices. Smear each slice with butter. Top two slices with the egg salad, dividing it evenly. Top with the remaining two bread slices, butter-side down. Cut each sandwich into three mini sandwiches and then serve.

Pizza Toast

Let's give this toaster-oven specialty a little respect and credibility. Pizza toast, the dressed-up cousin of cheese toast, is the hero of the late-night munchies, the star of homemade minimal-effort snack mash-ups. Use sauce if you have it, cheese of any kind, and toppings depending on what you have in the pantry or refrigerator. You can go big with prep or from concept to in-the-oven in 3 minutes.

I normally only think of pizza toast as something made at home, but in Japan there are small cafes called kissaten, often family run, serving tea, coffee, and snacks, maybe a curry. Pizza toast is a specialty in some of these, and no, I've never been in one, so I'm not a kissaten expert, but in the current popular imagination, kissaten are the spiritual home of Japanese pizza toasts, made from thick slabs of Shokupan, the Japanese milk bread that is in this book on page 175.

Pizza sauce is really easy: it's just tomatoes and salt. You can add chile flakes if you like spice. No cooking ahead of time, it cooks on the pizza toast (or traditional pizza) while it bakes. Take one 28-ounce can of best-quality crushed tomatoes, add 8 grams of fine sea salt, and blend with a spoon. It's ready to go. If your can is whole peeled tomatoes, pulse in a blender with the salt for just 1 second to blend, not more. I usually go heavy with sauce and let some of it soak in, and I slice the bread pretty thick.

For cheese I prefer fresher cheeses with good meltability, whether it's mozzarella, fontina, pepper Jack, cheddar, or even slices of American Meunster cheese. Blending cheeses is great. I also make pizza toast with sauce and grated Parmesan, adding the cheese after it bakes—this reminds me of the pizza toast that I made when I was young, using a green can of grocery store Parmesan that we kept around for spaghetti nights.

For pizza toast toppings, I love pepperoni, but I often look around for what's at hand for inspiration. Corn kernels and sweet peppers, for example, are a nice combination.

Lightly toast a thick slab of pan bread or Dutch-oven bread in a toaster oven, then lay on sauce and toppings. Try sauce both ways too: under the cheese or on top of the cheese for an "upside down" pizza. Bake at a high temperature in your regular oven or toast in your toaster oven until done.

CHAPTER 7
DUTCH-OVEN
LEVAIN RECIPES

This book introduces a new approach to making naturally leavened breads at home. I have you make a sourdough culture (I usually use the word *levain*) which you store in the refrigerator and then pluck pieces from to build a recipe-specific starter in three quick-to-make stages: morning, evening, and the next morning (the day of the dough mix). It takes quite a while for the cold culture to wake up—just as it took a couple days to restore the refrigerated levain in *Flour Water Salt Yeast*. Here, you begin a starter with a small amount of levain, white bread flour, and water; mix by hand and leave it out until the evening; add another small amount of flour and water; and mix it again. The next morning, do one more feeding of the starter and it will then be in good form to rise your bread in a dough that you mix 7 or 8 hours later the same day. The dough will rise for 4 to 5 hours, depending on climate and season, then you'll shape the loaf, refrigerate it overnight, and bake it the next morning. For a Saturday-morning bake, begin the starter on Thursday morning.

All this seems like much more work than it really is. You can go the easy and good route by using this book's recipes for same-day or overnight pan breads where you add 100 grams from the levain container that's in the fridge and bake into Dutch-oven loaves. Or you can go the sourdough route and use the recipe for Dutch-oven levain loaves. The flavor of these breads is fantastic. This three-stage starter buildup keeps it from being too sour, and the long overnight cold proof of the dough is like a flavor lab creating layer upon layer of bread magic.

These recipes make one Dutch-oven levain bread. If you want to double the batch size of levain dough to make two loaves, the first two starter feeds on Day 1 are the same. On Day 2, keeping the same ratio of retained starter to fresh flour and water, double the morning starter mix from what you make for a one-loaf batch (use 100 grams retained starter, 200 grams flour, and 200 grams water). Mix that final dough 7 to 8 hours after the starter feeding as usual and double the ingredient quantities.

There is just one exception to this Dutch-oven levain bread schedule. The Apple-Cider Levain Bread works really well with a first rise overnight.

Temperature Note

The starter buildup instructions pay particular attention to water temperature and room temperature, and the recipes offer water temp adjustments to go with seasonal changes. At a room temperature of 80°F / 27°C, the fermentation of the starter (or your final dough) will be much faster than at 70°F / 21°C, and you can compensate by using cooler water to slow it down for a while. The whole idea is to prevent the starter at any stage from over-fermenting, which will produce sour flavors, while still allowing it to have the right development to give a good rise to the bread. If you can keep the starter and your dough in a spot that's at 70°F / 21°C while they are fermenting, you can follow the primary recipe instructions for water temperature and timing.

Seasonal Adjustments

Even when the thermostat in my house is set at 70°F during the winter, many surfaces—floors, countertops, my dough bucket—are cooler than they are during the summer months. The bread dough knows that it's cold outside.

I mention seasonal differences throughout this book, but the effects are especially noticeable with the levain bread doughs, and they require some tweaking to compensate. These doughs move more slowly in winter than they do in summer, but you can get good results in any season with some easy adjustments.

For the Dutch-oven levain bread recipes, please apply the guidelines in the following chart to get optimal performance (for the rise and for flavor) from your sourdough.

SEASONAL ADJUSTMENTS FOR SOURDOUGH

		Summer	Winter
Starter, Day 1: Morning Feed	water temperature	75° to 80°F / 24° to 27°C	85°F / 29° C
Starter, Day 1: Evening Feed	water temperature	70°F / 21°C	85°F / 29°C
Starter, Day 2: Morning Feed	retained starter from previous feeding	50 to 60 grams	75 grams
	water temperature	90° to 95°F / 32° to 35°C	95°F / 35°C

In the summer, if your sourdough is over-fermenting and your bread tastes too sour, decrease the water temperature even more for each feeding.

COUNTRY BREAD, EIB-STYLE (WITH A WALNUT BREAD VARIATION)

Dutch oven

The name "country bread" is a translation of the French *pain de campagne*. In keeping with the French version, this loaf has a rustic look and a rougher blend of flours than a pure-white city bread. The flour blend of a country bread is up to the baker, and the leavening will be entirely or mostly from a levain. Very often, it will have a small amount of rye flour. It could have a toss of buckwheat for flavor (buckwheat has no gluten-forming proteins, so if you try it, just use a little bit for flavor), or it could be all stone-ground and sifted flour. It should be delicious, crusty, and the opposite of a fine white bread, like pain de mie.

The starter builds are quick, simple mixes that can be done in just a couple minutes. Everything about baking with a naturally leavened culture is more work than straight yeasted doughs; but if you embrace it, you will find the resulting bread to be worth the planning and extra 5 or 10 minutes of your time.

Three feeds to build up the starter allows the culture to create enough leavening power to give a good rise to the bread and a good balance of flavors without being too sour. I tried a million and one single- or two-feed starter builds for the mix using my refrigerated levain as the seed, and either the rise wasn't up to a par and it needed added yeast or the flavor was too sour. It's not enough to simply make the bread rise well. It should taste good too.

You can use this recipe as a model for other breads made with the same leavening but differing blends of flour (use the same weight of total flour that I have in this recipe). Maybe you have some stone-milled spelt, Sonora white, or emmer flour that you want to use in place of the whole wheat here, or you want no rye flour in the mix. Go for it. Adjust the amount of water in the dough up a bit if you increase the percentage of whole-grain flour, and decrease the water if you go the other way. It helps a lot if you have made the recipe a few times before switching up the flour blend, to know what the dough consistency is supposed to feel like.

THIS RECIPE MAKES 1 DUTCH-OVEN LOAF OF ABOUT 2 POUNDS.

Please refer to the Seasonal Adjustments for Sourdough on page 187 for summer/winter changes.

First rise
About 5 hours at 70°F / 21°C room temperature,
maybe 4 hours in summer.

Proof time
Overnight in the refrigerator.

Bake
Preheat to 475°F / 245°C for 45 minutes,
bake at 475°F / 245°C for about 50 minutes.

Sample schedule
Day 1, morning (*between 8 a.m. and noon*): Mix starter. Let sit out.

Day 1, evening (*8 to 12 hours later*): Second mix of starter. Let sit out.

Day 2, morning (*10 to 12 hours after previous night's mix*):
Mix starter again. Let sit out.

Day 2, afternoon (*7 to 8 hours after starter was mixed*):
Final dough mix. Give it three folds. Rise time is about 4 hours in summer,
5 hours in winter.

Day 2, evening: Remove dough from tub, shape loaf,
let proof overnight in refrigerator.

Day 3, morning to early afternoon: Bake.

STARTER: DAY 1, MORNING (between 8 a.m. and noon)

Ingredient	Quantity
Levain	50 to 60 g / ¼ cup
White bread flour	100 g / ½ cup + 3 Tbsp + 1¼ tsp
Water (75° to 80°F / 24° to 27°C; summer) (85°F / 29°C; winter)	100 g / ¼ cup + 2 Tbsp + 2 tsp

STARTER: DAY 1, EVENING (8 to 12 hours later)

Ingredient	Quantity
Morning starter mix	All of it
White bread flour	100 g / ½ cup + 3 Tbsp + 1¼ tsp
Water (70°F / 21°C; summer) (85°F / 29°C; winter)	100 g / ¼ cup + 2 Tbsp + 2 tsp

STARTER: DAY 2, MORNING (10 to 12 hours after previous night's mix)

Ingredient	Quantity
Starter	50 to 60 g / ¼ cup (summer) 75 g / ¼ cup + 2 Tbsp (winter)
White bread flour	100 g / ½ cup + 3 Tbsp + 1¼ tsp
Water (90° to 95°F / 32° to 35°C)	100 g / ¼ cup + 2 Tbsp + 2 tsp

FINAL DOUGH: DAY 2, AFTERNOON (7 to 8 hours after starter was mixed; 6 hours works if you keep the starter at 80° to 85°F / 27° to 29°C)

Ingredient	Quantity	Baker's Percentage
White bread flour*	295 g / 2 cups + 1 Tbsp + 2¼ tsp	79%
Whole-wheat flour*	80 g / ½ cup + 1 Tbsp + ½ tsp	16%
Whole or dark rye flour*	25 g / 3 Tbsp + ¼ tsp	5%
Water (90° to 95°F / 32° to 35°C)	300 g / 1¼ cups	80%**
Fine sea salt	11 g / 2¼ tsp	2.2%
Starter*	200 g / 1 cup	20%
Roasted walnut pieces (optional; see variation)	115 g / 1¼ cups	23%

* Total flour includes flour in starter = 500 grams

** Includes water in starter

■ DAY 1, MORNING (between 8 a.m. and noon)

To begin the starter, weigh a 2-quart container with a lid (or a big bowl) while it's empty (without lid) and mark its weight on the container's side or write it down. You will need this info later.

Measure 100 grams (75° to 80°F / 24° to 27°C) water into your container. Add 50 to 60 grams levain from the refrigerator and stir a bit with your fingers to loosen up the culture. Add 100 grams white bread flour and mix with your fingers until all is incorporated.

Cover with the lid or plastic wrap and leave it out at room temperature. This works well at 70°F / 21°C room temperature. (If your kitchen is much warmer than that, e.g., 75° to 80°F / 24° to 27°C, use cooler water at 65° to 70°F / 18° to 21°C.) Put the levain back into the fridge.

■ DAY 1, EVENING (8 to 12 hours later)

Retain all the morning starter mix. Measure 100 grams (70°F / 21°C) water and 100 grams white bread flour into the same container on top of your first starter mix. Mix with your fingers until all is incorporated.

Cover with the lid or plastic wrap and leave it out at room temperature (65° to 70°F / 18° to 21°C) until the next morning. If it is summer and your kitchen is much warmer than that through the night, e.g., 75° to 80°F / 24° to 27°C, use cooler water again, this time about 60°F / 16°C. (Cooler than before because the rest of the starter is already at a warm room temperature.)

■ DAY 2, MORNING (10 to 12 hours after previous night's mix)

Around 8 a.m., reference the empty container weight and remove all but 50 to 60 grams of the Day 1 starter from your container. (Use the extra to make the excellent pizza dough on page 237, or toss it.) Measure 100 grams (95°F / 35°C) water into the container with the starter and mix with your fingers until you have a slurry. Add 100 grams white bread flour. Mix with your fingers until all is incorporated. Keep in a warm place, 70° to 75°F / 21° to 24°C.

■ DAY 2, AFTERNOON (7 to 8 hours after starter was mixed)

Do a final dough mix using the following instructions. A visual cue that the starter is ready for this next phase is that at a certain point, there will be some small bubbles at the top. About an hour later, the whole top will be covered in little bubbles. It is at this second bubbly stage that the starter is ready. You will feel its light and gassy texture when you remove it to put it into your final dough mix. It will remain usable for a couple hours before starting to develop more sour flavors.

1. Autolyse

Measure 300 grams (90° to 95°F / 32° to 35°C) water into a 6-quart round tub or similar container. Use a wet hand (so it doesn't stick) to add 200 grams of the Day 2 starter you mixed in the morning. Stir a bit with your fingers to loosen up the culture. Add 295 grams white bread flour, 80 grams whole-wheat flour, and 25 grams rye flour. Mix it by hand until all is incorporated.

Sprinkle 11 grams fine sea salt evenly across the top of the autolyse dough. Let it rest there, where it will partially dissolve.

Cover and let rest for 20 minutes.

2. Mix

Mix by hand, wetting your working hand before mixing so the dough doesn't stick to you. Reach underneath the dough and grab about one-fourth of it. Gently stretch this section and fold it over the top to the other side of the dough. Repeat three more times with the remaining dough until the salt is fully enclosed.

Use the pincer method to fully integrate the ingredients. Make five or six pincer cuts across the entire mass of dough. Then fold the dough over itself a few times. Repeat, alternately cutting and folding, until all the ingredients are fully integrated. Let the dough rest for a few minutes, then fold for another 30 seconds or until the dough tightens up. The whole process should take about 5 minutes. The target dough temperature at the end of the mix is 75° to 80°F / 24° to 27°C. Cover the tub and let the dough rise until the next fold.

3. Fold & First Rise

This dough needs three folds (see page 41). It's easiest to apply the folds during the first 1½ hours after mixing the dough. Apply the first fold about 10 minutes after mixing and the second and third when you see the dough spread out in the tub from the previous fold. If need be, it's okay to fold later; just be sure to leave it alone for the last hour of rising.

When the dough is about two and a half times its original volume, and the edge of the dough is about ½ inch below the 2-quart line in the dough tub, it's ready to be made up into a loaf. If it is in a room at 70°F / 21°C, this first ferment should take 4 to 5 hours. It will happen faster in summer, so keep an eye on the volume expansion to make the call. Judge when it's ready based on volume expansion more than time. (If your kitchen is warmer or colder than mine, your time will vary.) If you're not using a marked dough tub, you'll have to eyeball it. Use your best judgment.

■ **DAY 2, EVENING**

4. Remove the Dough from Its Tub

Lightly flour a work surface about 12 inches wide. Flour your hands and sprinkle a bit of flour around the edges of the tub. Tip the tub slightly and gently work your floured free hand beneath the dough to loosen it from the bottom of the tub. Then turn the tub on its side and ease the dough out onto the work surface without pulling or tearing it.

5. Shape

Dust a proofing basket moderately with flour and spread the flour around with your hand. Shape the dough into a medium-tight ball following the instructions on pages 47 to 49. Place it seam-side down in its proofing basket.

6. Proof

Place the basket in a nonperforated plastic bag, tuck the bag under the basket, and refrigerate overnight.

The next morning, 12 to 16 hours after the loaf went into the refrigerator, it should be ready to bake, straight from the refrigerator. It does not need to come to room temperature first.

■ DAY 3, MORNING TO EARLY AFTERNOON

7. Preheat

About 45 minutes prior to baking, position a rack in the middle of the oven and put a Dutch oven, with its lid, on the rack. Preheat the oven to 475°F / 245°C.

8. Bake

For the next step, please be careful not to let your hands, fingers, or forearms touch the extremely hot Dutch oven.

Invert the basket with its proofed loaf onto a lightly floured countertop, keeping in mind that the top of the loaf will be the side that was facing down while it was rising—the seam side. Give the basket a firm tap on the countertop to pop the dough out.

Use oven mitts to remove the preheated Dutch oven from your oven, remove the lid, and carefully place the loaf, seam-side up, in the hot Dutch oven. Use the mitts to replace the lid, return the Dutch oven to the center of the middle rack, and bake for 30 minutes. Then carefully remove the lid and bake for about 20 minutes more, until dark brown all around the loaf. Check after 15 minutes of baking uncovered in case your oven runs hot.

Remove the Dutch oven and carefully tilt it to turn the loaf out. Let the loaf cool on a rack or set on its side, so air can circulate around it, for 20 minutes before slicing.

> **BAKING NOTE**
> **If you have had problems with the bottom of your loaf scorching, it's because your oven heats from the bottom and is applying too much heat to the underside of your Dutch oven. Set up a heat shield as described on page 52.**

WALNUT BREAD

You really need to give this a try. Eating walnut bread with honey and butter should make you pause, put down the phone, and just go to that special place in your imagination where the unicorns live.

One hour before mixing the dough, lightly roast the walnuts. Preheat the oven to 350°F / 180°C. Measure 115 grams walnut pieces and spread them evenly across a baking sheet or ovenproof skillet. Roast for 6 or 7 minutes, making sure not to take them too dark. Let cool at room temperature.

For the dough mix, go ahead and add the cooled roasted walnuts to the flour, water, and levain that make up the Autolyse step. It's much easier to have the nuts integrate evenly through the dough this way. All the remaining recipe steps are the same.

Bake Like Your Ancestors

The human cultivation of wheat was a golden-spike moment in the development of agrarian society, and it produced the planet's first bread bakers. For most of human history, this is the only way that leavened bread was made—from a mixture of mashed-up grains (flour) and water that ultimately, when left out for some time, starts to ferment. This naturally fermented mash made the bread of history, the way it was for most of our bread-eating existence. It made beer too! Liquid bread.

There are two planting periods for our wheat crops, autumn and spring, yet one harvest period in late summer for both winter wheat and spring wheat. Thousands of varieties are farmed from south to north, replaced mostly by rye in farther-north climes. The harvest, bushels of wheat berries threshed from the fields, can be stored year-round and milled as needed. Bread was once essential for survival in a way we just can't imagine anymore.

Mills were mostly local and powered by water or wind. Bakers were an important part of the community. Here's your chance to connect to the past and have it taste good!

PAIN AU LEVAIN

Dutch oven

This is an all-white-flour levain bread without added yeast. The lighter taste of white wheat flour allows the flavors from this dough's natural fermentation to take center stage. The white flour starter has fruity, lactic flavors to add to the bread, and the feeding schedule keeps it mellow but strong enough to give this loaf a good rise.

I especially like this bread toasted and topped with butter and preserves; for grilled cheese or cheese toast, beans and salsa on toast, and poached egg on toast; for thick-sliced garlic bread; and as grilled hunks for using as dippers or trenchers for winter and summer stews.

THIS RECIPE MAKES 1 DUTCH-OVEN LOAF OF ABOUT 2 POUNDS.

Please refer to the Seasonal Adjustments for Sourdough on page 187 for summer/winter changes.

First rise
About 5 hours at 70°F / 21°C room temperature,
maybe 4 hours in summer.

Proof time
Overnight in the refrigerator.

Bake
Preheat to 475°F / 245°C for 45 minutes,
bake at 475°F / 245°C for about 50 minutes.

Sample schedule
Day 1, morning (*between 8 a.m. and noon*): Mix starter. Let sit out.

Day 1, evening (*8 to 12 hours later*): Second mix of starter. Let sit out.

Day 2, morning (*10 to 12 hours after previous night's mix*):
Mix starter again. Let sit out.

Day 2, afternoon (*7 to 8 hours after starter was mixed*): Final dough
mix. Give dough three folds. Rise time is about 4 hours in summer,
5 hours in winter.

Day 2, evening: Remove dough from tub, shape loaf,
let proof overnight in refrigerator.

Day 3, morning to early afternoon: Bake.

STARTER: DAY 1, MORNING (between 8 a.m. and noon)

Ingredient	Quantity
Levain	50 to 60 g / ¼ cup
White bread flour	100 g / ½ cup + 3 Tbsp + 1¼ tsp
Water (75° to 80°F / 24° to 27°C; summer) (85°F / 29°C; winter)	100 g / ¼ cup + 2 Tbsp + 2 tsp

STARTER: DAY 1, EVENING (8 to 12 hours later)

Ingredient	Quantity
Morning starter mix	All of it
White bread flour	100 g / ½ cup + 3 Tbsp + 1¼ tsp
Water (70°F / 21°C; summer) (85°F / 29°C; winter)	100 g / ¼ cup + 2 Tbsp + 2 tsp

STARTER: DAY 2, MORNING (10 to 12 hours after previous night's mix)

Ingredient	Quantity
Starter	50 to 60 g / ¼ cup (summer) 75 g / ¼ cup + 2 Tbsp (winter)
White bread flour	100 g / ½ cup + 3 Tbsp + 1¼ tsp
Water (90° to 95°F / 32° to 35°C)	100 g / ¼ cup + 2 Tbsp + 2 tsp

FINAL DOUGH: DAY 2, AFTERNOON (7 to 8 hours after starter was mixed; 6 hours works if you keep the starter at 80° to 85°F / 27° to 29°C)

Ingredient	Quantity	Baker's Percentage
White bread flour*	400 g / 2¾ cups + 2 tsp	100%
Water (90° to 95°F / 32° to 35°C)	270 g / 1 cup + 3 Tbsp	74%**
Fine sea salt	11 g / 2¼ tsp	2.2%
Starter*	200 g / 1 cup	20%

* Total flour includes flour in starter = 500 grams

** Includes water in starter

DAY 1, MORNING (between 8 a.m. and noon)

To begin the starter, weigh a 2-quart container with a lid (or a big bowl) while it's empty (without lid) and mark its weight on the container's side or write it down. You will need this info later.

Measure 100 grams (75° to 80°F / 24° to 27°C) water into your container. Add 50 to 60 grams levain from the refrigerator and stir a bit with your fingers to loosen up the culture. Add 100 grams white bread flour and mix with your fingers until all is incorporated.

Cover with the lid or plastic wrap and leave it out at room temperature. This works well at 70°F / 21°C room temperature. (If your kitchen is much warmer than that, e.g., 75° to 80°F / 24° to 27°C, use cooler water at 65° to 70°F / 18° to 21°C.)

DAY 1, EVENING (8 to 12 hours later)

Retain all the morning starter mix. Measure 100 grams (70°F / 21°C) water and 100 grams white bread flour into the same container on top of your first starter mix. Mix with your fingers until all is incorporated.

Cover with the lid or plastic wrap and leave it out at room temperature (65° to 70°F / 18° to 21°C) until the next morning. If it is summer and your kitchen is much warmer than that through the night, e.g., 75° to 80°F / 24° to 27°C, use cooler water again, this time about 60°F / 16°C. (Cooler than before because the rest of the starter is already at a warm room temperature.)

DAY 2, MORNING (10 to 12 hours after previous night's mix)

Around 8 a.m., reference the empty container weight and remove all but 50 to 60 grams of the Day 1 starter from your container. (Use the extra to make the excellent pizza dough on page 237, or toss it.) Measure 100 grams (95°F / 35°C) water into the container with the starter and mix with your fingers until you have a slurry. Add 100 grams white bread flour. Mix with your fingers until all is incorporated. Keep in a warm place, 70° to 75°F / 21° to 24°C.

DAY 2, AFTERNOON (7 to 8 hours after starter was mixed)

Do a final dough mix using the following instructions. A visual cue that the starter is ready for this next phase is that at a certain point, there will be some small bubbles at the top. About an hour later, the whole top will be covered in little bubbles. It is at this second bubbly stage that the starter is ready. You will feel its light and gassy texture when you remove it to put it into your final dough mix. It will remain usable for a couple of hours before starting to develop more sour flavors.

1. Autolyse

Measure 270 grams (90° to 95°F / 32° to 35°C) water into a 6-quart round tub or similar container. Use a wet hand (so it doesn't stick) to add 200 grams of the Day 2 starter you mixed in the morning. Stir a bit with your fingers to loosen up the culture. Add 400 grams white bread flour. Mix it by hand until all is incorporated.

Sprinkle 11 grams fine sea salt evenly across the top of the autolyse dough. Let it rest there, where it will partially dissolve.

Cover and let rest for 20 minutes.

2. Mix

Mix by hand, wetting your working hand before mixing so the dough doesn't stick to you. Reach underneath the dough and grab about one-fourth of it. Gently stretch this section and fold it over the top to the other side of the dough. Repeat three more times with the remaining dough until the salt is fully enclosed.

Use the pincer method to fully integrate the ingredients. Make five or six pincer cuts across the entire mass of dough. Then fold the dough over itself a few times. Repeat, alternately cutting and folding, until all the ingredients are fully integrated. Let the dough rest for a few minutes, then fold for another 30 seconds or until the dough tightens up. The whole process should take about 5 minutes. The target dough temperature at the end of the mix is 75° to 80°F / 24° to 27°C. Cover the tub and let the dough rise until the next fold.

3. Fold & First Rise

This dough needs three folds (see page 41). It's easiest to apply the folds during the first 1½ hours after mixing the dough. Apply the first fold about 10 minutes after mixing and the second and third when you see the dough spread out in the tub from the previous fold. If need be, it's okay to fold later; just be sure to leave it alone for the last hour of rising.

When the dough is about two and a half times its original volume, and the edge of the dough is about ½ inch below the 2-quart line in the dough tub, it's ready to be made up into a loaf. If it is in a room at 70°F / 21°C, this first ferment should take 4 to 5 hours. It will happen faster in summer, so keep an eye on the volume expansion to make the call. Judge when it's ready based on volume expansion more than time. (If your kitchen is warmer or colder than mine, your time will vary.) If you're not using a marked dough tub, you'll have to eyeball it. Use your best judgment.

■ **DAY 2, EVENING**

4. Remove the Dough from Its Tub

Lightly flour a work surface about 12 inches wide. Flour your hands and sprinkle a bit of flour around the edges of the tub. Tip the tub slightly and gently work your floured free hand beneath the dough to loosen it from the bottom of the tub. Then turn the tub on its side and ease the dough out onto the work surface without pulling or tearing it.

5. Shape

Dust a proofing basket moderately with flour and spread the flour around with your hand. Shape the dough into a medium-tight ball following the instructions on pages 47 to 49. Place it seam-side down in its proofing basket.

6. Proof

Place the basket in a nonperforated plastic bag, tuck the bag under the basket, and refrigerate overnight.

The next morning, 12 to 16 hours after the loaf went into the refrigerator, it should be ready to bake, straight from the refrigerator. It does not need to come to room temperature first.

■ DAY 3, MORNING TO EARLY AFTERNOON

7. Preheat

About 45 minutes prior to baking, position a rack in the middle of the oven and put a Dutch oven, with its lid, on the rack. Preheat the oven to 475°F / 245°C.

8. Bake

For the next step, please be careful not to let your hands, fingers, or forearms touch the extremely hot Dutch oven.

Invert the basket with its proofed loaf onto a lightly floured countertop, keeping in mind that the top of the loaf will be the side that was facing down while it was rising—the seam side. Give the basket a firm tap on the countertop to pop the dough out.

Use oven mitts to remove the preheated Dutch oven from your oven, remove the lid, and carefully place the loaf, seam-side up, in the hot Dutch oven. Use the mitts to replace the lid, return the Dutch oven to the center of the middle rack, and bake for 30 minutes. Then carefully remove the lid and bake for about 20 minutes more, until dark brown all around the loaf. Check after 15 minutes of baking uncovered in case your oven runs hot.

Remove the Dutch oven and carefully tilt it to turn the loaf out. Let the loaf cool on a rack or set on its side, so air can circulate around it, for 20 minutes before slicing.

50% EMMER OR EINKORN DUTCH-OVEN LEVAIN BREAD

Dutch oven

Here's an essential take on stone-milled "craft flour" bread-baking at home. In place of emmer or einkorn stone-milled whole-grain flour, you could also use some of the heirloom wheat varieties available from many of the same mills. Spelt flour would be good too. The flavor and texture of this bread is so good; it might become your favorite recipe in this book.

The pan breads can tolerate a little more water in the dough than Dutch-oven loaves, as they have the pan to provide physical support to keep them from spreading out. But a bigger deal to me as I tested super-wet doughs for Dutch-oven baking is that the dough was likely to stick to my wicker proofing basket by the time I was ready to remove it for baking. There is too much time and anticipation in this whole process for a fail point in the last step, so I do not recommend increasing dough hydration on this recipe if you are proofing in wicker baskets as I like to do.

Einkorn levain bread makes superb thick-cut French toast; if you haven't thought about it, I highly recommend a savory French toast—add grated Parmesan, for example, to an eggy soak, along with some finely chopped celery, peppers, herbs, bacon, or whatever else you want. Thick cuts are the way to go with this bread. It also makes a fantastic grilled cheese or grilled bread topped with any spread you want to smear on it.

THIS RECIPE MAKES 1 DUTCH-OVEN LOAF OF ABOUT 2 POUNDS.

Please refer to the Seasonal Adjustments for Sourdough on page 187 for summer/winter changes.

First rise
About 5 hours at 70°F / 21°C room temperature,
maybe 4 hours in summer.

Proof time
Overnight in the refrigerator.

Bake
Preheat to 475°F / 245°C for 45 minutes,
bake at 475°F / 245°C for about 50 minutes.

Sample schedule
Day 1, morning (*between 8 a.m. and noon*): Mix starter. Let sit out.

Day 1, evening (*8 to 12 hours later*): Second mix of starter. Let sit out.

Day 2, morning (*10 to 12 hours after previous night's mix*):
Mix starter again. Let sit out.

Day 2, afternoon (*7 to 8 hours after starter was mixed*): Final dough
mix. Give dough three folds. Rise time is about 4 hours in summer,
5 hours in winter.

Day 2, evening: Remove dough from tub, shape loaf,
let proof overnight in refrigerator.

Day 3, morning to early afternoon: Bake.

STARTER: DAY 1, MORNING (between 8 a.m. and noon)

Ingredient	Quantity
Levain	50 to 60 g / ¼ cup
White Bread Flour	100 g / ½ cup + 3 Tbsp + 1¼ tsp
Water (75° to 80°F / 24° to 27°C; summer) (85°F / 29°C; winter)	100 g / ¼ cup + 2 Tbsp + 2 tsp

STARTER: DAY 2, MORNING (10 to 12 hours after previous night's mix)

Ingredient	Quantity
Morning starter mix	All of it
White bread flour	100 g / ½ cup + 3 Tbsp + 1¼ tsp
Water (70°F / 21°C; summer) (85°F / 29°C; winter)	100 g / ¼ cup + 2 Tbsp + 2 tsp

STARTER: DAY 2, MORNING (10 to 12 hours after previous night's mix)

Ingredient	Quantity
Starter	50 to 60 g / ¼ cup (summer) 75 g / ¼ cup + 2 Tbsp (winter)
White bread flour	100 g / ½ cup + 3 Tbsp + 1¼ tsp
Water (90° to 95°F / 32° to 35°C)	100 g / ¼ cup + 2 Tbsp + 2 tsp

FINAL DOUGH: DAY 2, AFTERNOON (7 to 8 hours after starter was mixed; 6 hours works if you keep the starter at 80° to 85°F / 27° to 29°C)

Ingredient	Quantity	Baker's Percentage
White bread flour*	150 g / 1 cup + 2 Tbsp + 2¼ tsp	50%
Whole-grain emmer or einkorn flour*	250 g / 1¾ cups + 1¾ tsp	50%
Water (90° to 95°F / 32° to 35°C)	310 g / 1⅓ cups	82%**
Fine sea salt	11 g / 2¼ tsp	2.2%
Starter*	200 g / 1 cup	20%

* Total flour includes flour in the starter = 500 g

** Includes water in starter

DAY 1, MORNING (between 8 a.m. and noon)

To begin the starter, weigh a 2-quart container with a lid (or a big bowl) while it's empty (without lid) and mark its weight on the container's side or write it down. You will need this info later.

Measure 100 grams (75° to 80°F / 24° to 27°C) water into your container. Add 50 to 60 grams levain from the refrigerator and stir a bit with your fingers to loosen up the culture. Add 100 grams white bread flour and mix with your fingers until all is incorporated.

Cover with the lid or plastic wrap and leave it out at room temperature. This works well at 70°F / 21°C room temperature. (If your kitchen is much warmer than that, e.g., 75° to 80°F / 24° to 27°C, use cooler water at 65° to 70°F / 18° to 21°C.) Put the levain back into the fridge.

DAY 1, EVENING (8 to 12 hours later)

Retain all the morning starter mix. Measure 100 grams (70°F / 21°C) water and 100 grams white bread flour into the same container on top of your first starter mix. Mix with your fingers until all is incorporated.

Cover with the lid or plastic wrap and leave it out at room temperature (65° to 70°F / 18° to 21°C) until the next morning. If it is summer and your kitchen is much warmer than that through the night, e.g., 75° to 80°F / 24° to 27°C, use cooler water again, this time about 60°F / 16°C. (Cooler than before because the rest of the starter is already at a warm room temperature.)

DAY 2, MORNING (10 to 12 hours after previous night's mix)

Around 8 a.m., reference the empty container weight and remove all but 50 to 60 grams of the Day 1 starter from your container. (Use the extra to make the excellent pizza dough on page 237, or toss it.) Measure 100 grams (95°F / 35°C) water into the container with the starter and mix with your fingers until you have a slurry. Add 100 grams white bread flour. Mix with your fingers until all is incorporated. Keep in a warm place, 70° to 75°F / 21° to 24°C.

DAY 2, AFTERNOON (7 to 8 hours after starter was mixed)

Do a final dough mix using the following instructions. A visual cue that the starter is ready for this next phase is that at a certain point, there will be some small bubbles at the top. About an hour later, the whole top will be covered in little bubbles. It is at this second bubbly stage that the starter is ready. You will feel its light and gassy texture when you remove it to put it into your final dough mix. It will remain usable for a couple of hours before starting to develop more sour flavors.

1. Autolyse

Measure 310 grams (90° to 95°F / 32° to 35°C) water into a 6-quart round tub or similar container. Use a wet hand (so it doesn't stick) to add 200 grams of the Day 2 starter you mixed in the morning. Stir a bit with your fingers to loosen up the culture. Add 150 grams white bread flour and 250 grams whole-grain emmer or einkorn flour. Mix it by hand until all is incorporated.

Sprinkle 11 grams fine sea salt evenly across the top of the autolyse dough. Let it rest there, where it will partially dissolve.

Cover and let rest for 20 to 30 minutes.

2. Mix

Mix by hand, wetting your working hand before mixing so the dough doesn't stick to you. Reach underneath the dough and grab about one-fourth of it. Gently stretch this section and fold it over the top to the other side of the dough. Repeat three more times with the remaining dough until the salt is fully enclosed.

Use the pincer method to fully integrate the ingredients. Make five or six pincer cuts across the entire mass of dough. Then fold the dough over itself a few times. Repeat, alternately cutting and folding, until all the ingredients are fully integrated. Let the dough rest for a few minutes, then fold for another 30 seconds or until the dough tightens up. The whole process should take about 5 minutes. The target dough temperature at the end of the mix is 75° to 80°F / 24° to 27°C. Cover the tub and let the dough rise until the next fold.

3. Fold & First Rise

This dough needs three folds (see page 41). It's easiest to apply the folds during the 1½ hours after mixing the dough. Apply the first fold about 10 minutes after mixing and the second and third when you see the dough spread out in the tub from the previous fold. If need be, it's okay to fold later; just be sure to leave it alone for the last hour of rising.

When the dough is about two and a half times its original volume, and the edge of the dough is about ½ inch below the 2-quart line in the dough tub, it's ready to be made up into a loaf. If it is in a room at 70°F / 21°C, this first ferment should take 4 to 5 hours. It will happen faster in summer, so keep an eye on the volume expansion to make the call. Judge when it's ready based on volume expansion more than time. (If your kitchen is warmer or colder than mine, your time will vary.) If you're not using a marked dough tub, you'll have to eyeball it. Use your best judgment.

■ **DAY 2, EVENING**

4. Remove the Dough from Its Tub

Lightly flour a work surface about 12 inches wide. Flour your hands and sprinkle a bit of flour around the edges of the tub. Tip the tub slightly and gently work your floured free hand beneath the dough to loosen it from the bottom of the tub. Then turn the tub on its side and ease the dough out onto the work surface without pulling or tearing it.

5. Shape

Dust a proofing basket moderately with flour and spread the flour around with your hand. Shape the dough into a medium-tight ball following the instructions on pages 47 to 49. Place it seam-side down in its proofing basket.

6. Proof

Place the basket in a nonperforated plastic bag, tuck the bag under the basket, and refrigerate overnight.

The next morning, 12 to 16 hours after the loaf went into the refrigerator, it should be ready to bake, straight from the refrigerator. It does not need to come to room temperature first.

■ DAY 3, MORNING TO EARLY AFTERNOON

7. Preheat

About 45 minutes prior to baking, position a rack in the middle of the oven and put a Dutch oven, with its lid, on the rack. Preheat the oven to 475°F / 245°C.

8. Bake

For the next step, please be careful not to let your hands, fingers, or forearms touch the extremely hot Dutch oven.

Invert the basket with its proofed loaf onto a lightly floured countertop, keeping in mind that the top of the loaf will be the side that was facing down while it was rising—the seam side. Give the basket a firm tap on the countertop to pop the dough out.

Use oven mitts to remove the preheated Dutch oven from your oven, remove the lid, and carefully place the loaf, seam-side up, in the hot Dutch oven. Use the mitts to replace the lid, return the Dutch oven to the center of the middle rack, and bake for 30 minutes. Then carefully remove the lid and bake for about 20 minutes more, until dark brown all around the loaf. Check after 15 minutes of baking uncovered in case your oven runs hot.

Remove the Dutch oven and carefully tilt it to turn the loaf out. Let the loaf cool on a rack or set on its side, so air can circulate around it, for 20 minutes before slicing.

FIELD BLEND #3

Dutch oven

We made nearly this bread—a field blend of whole-wheat, whole rye, and white bread flour—for six years at Trifecta Tavern & Bakery in Portland and proofed the loaves in round wicker baskets like the one I recommend for this book's recipes. The levain bread doughs at Trifecta were mixed at around 7 a.m. and made up into loaves around noon; then they would go into the refrigerator to slow proof overnight at 37°F / 3°C, to be baked the next day at around 6 a.m.

This is the bread that I wanted to go with the oysters we served at Trifecta, and I can taste it now with the briny bounce of a half dozen Shigokus and our house-made butter. Great with a martini. I miss that place.

For home use, I like hunks of this bread rewarmed to a crisp outer shell and a still-soft, warm center to go with soups or anything brothy. It's also excellent with roast chicken and versatile for sandwiches, cheese toast, honey butter, dog snacks, and croutons.

THIS RECIPE MAKES 1 DUTCH-OVEN LOAF OF ABOUT 2 POUNDS.

Please refer to the Seasonal Adjustments for Sourdough on page 187 for summer/winter changes.

First rise
About 5 hours at 70°F / 21°C room temperature,
maybe 4 hours in summer.

Proof time
Overnight in the refrigerator.

Bake
Preheat to 475°F / 245°C for 45 minutes,
bake at 475°F / 245°C about 50 minutes.

Sample schedule
Day 1, morning (*between 8 a.m. and noon*): Mix starter. Let sit out.

Day 1, evening (*8 to 12 hours later*): Second mix of starter. Let sit out.

Day 2, morning (*10 to 12 hours after previous night's mix*):
Mix starter again. Let sit out.

Day 2, afternoon (*7 to 8 hours after starter was mixed*): Final dough mix.
Give dough three folds. Rise time is about 4 hours in summer,
5 hours in winter.

Day 2, evening: Remove dough from tub, shape loaf,
let proof overnight in refrigerator.

Day 3, morning to early afternoon: Bake.

STARTER: DAY 1, MORNING (between 8 a.m. and noon)

Ingredient	Quantity
Levain	50 to 60 g / ¼ cup
White bread flour	100 g / ½ cup + 3 Tbsp + 1¼ tsp
Water (75° to 80°F / 24° to 27°C; summer) (85°F / 29°C; winter)	100 g / ¼ cup + 2 Tbsp + 2 tsp

STARTER: DAY 1, EVENING (8 to 12 hours later)

Ingredient	Quantity
Morning starter mix	All of it
White bread flour	100 g / ½ cup + 3 Tbsp + 1¼ tsp
Water (70°F / 21°C; summer) (85°F / 29°C; winter)	100 g / ¼ cup + 2 Tbsp + 2 tsp

STARTER: DAY 2, MORNING (10 to 12 hours after previous night's mix)

Ingredient	Quantity
Starter	50 to 60 g / ¼ cup (summer) 75 g / ¼ cup + 2 Tbsp (winter)
White bread flour	100 g / ½ cup + 3 Tbsp + 1¼ tsp
Water (90° to 95°F / 32° to 35°C)	100 g / ¼ cup + 2 Tbsp + 2 tsp

FINAL DOUGH: DAY 2, AFTERNOON (7 to 8 hours after starter was mixed; 6 hours works if you keep the starter at 80° to 85°F / 27° to 29°C)

Ingredient	Quantity	Baker's Percentage
White bread flour*	200 g / 1¼ cups + 2 Tbsp + 2½ tsp	60%
Whole or dark rye flour*	115 g / ¾ cup + 2 Tbsp + ½ tsp	23%
Whole-wheat flour*	85 g / ½ cup + 1 Tbsp + 2¼ tsp	17%
Water (90° to 95°F / 32° to 35°C)	310 g / 1¼ cups + 2 tsp	82%**
Fine sea salt	11 g / 2¼ tsp	2.2%
Starter*	200 g / 1 cup	20%

* Total flour includes flour in starter = 500 grams

** Includes water in starter

■ DAY 1, MORNING (between 8 a.m. and noon)

To begin the starter, weigh a 2-quart container with a lid (or a big bowl) while it's empty (without lid) and mark its weight on the container's side or write it down. You will need this info later.

Measure 100 grams (75° to 80°F / 24° to 27°C) water into your container. Add 50 to 60 grams levain from the refrigerator and stir a bit with your fingers to loosen up the culture. Add 100 grams white bread flour and mix with your fingers until all is incorporated.

Cover with the lid or plastic wrap and leave it out at room temperature. This works well at 70°F / 21°C room temperature. (If your kitchen is much warmer than that, e.g., 75° to 80°F / 24° to 27°C, use cooler water at 65° to 70°F / 18° to 21°C.) Put the levain back into the fridge.

■ DAY 1, EVENING (8 to 12 hours later)

Retain all the morning starter mix. Measure 100 grams (70°F / 21°C) water and 100 grams white bread flour into the same container on top of your first starter mix. Mix with your fingers until all is incorporated.

Cover with the lid or plastic wrap and leave it out at room temperature (65° to 70°F / 18° to 21°C) until the next morning. If it is summer and your kitchen is much warmer than that through the night, e.g., 75° to 80°F / 24° to 27°C, use cooler water again, this time about 60°F / 16°C. (Cooler than before because the rest of the starter is already at a warm room temperature.)

▌ DAY 2, MORNING (10 to 12 hours after previous night's mix)

Around 8 a.m., reference the empty container weight and remove all but 50 to 60 grams of the Day 1 starter from your container. (Use the extra to make the excellent pizza dough on page 237, or toss it.) Measure 100 grams (95°F / 35°C) water into the container with the starter and mix with your fingers until you have a slurry. Add 100 grams white bread flour. Mix with your fingers until all is incorporated. Keep in a warm place, 70° to 75°F / 21° to 24°C.

▌ DAY 2, AFTERNOON (7 to 8 hours after starter was mixed)

Do a final dough mix using the following instructions. A visual cue that the starter is ready for this next phase is that at a certain point, there will be some small bubbles at the top. About an hour later, the whole top will be covered in little bubbles. It is at this second bubbly stage that the starter is ready. You will feel its light and gassy texture when you remove it to put it into your final dough mix. It will remain usable for a couple of hours before starting to develop more sour flavors.

1. Autolyse

Measure 310 grams (90° to 95°F / 32° to 35°C) water into a 6-quart round tub or similar container. Use a wet hand (so it doesn't stick) to add 200 grams of the Day 2 starter you mixed in the morning. Stir a bit with your fingers to loosen up the culture. Add 200 grams white bread flour, 115 grams rye flour, and 85 grams whole-wheat flour. Mix it by hand until all is incorporated.

Sprinkle 11 grams fine sea salt evenly across the top of the autolyse dough. Let it rest there, where it will partially dissolve.

Cover and let rest for 20 to 30 minutes.

2. Mix

Mix by hand, wetting your working hand before mixing so the dough doesn't stick to you. Reach underneath the dough and grab about one-fourth of it. Gently stretch this section and fold it over the top to the other side of the dough. Repeat three more times with the remaining dough until the salt is fully enclosed. (You'll notice the rye dough doesn't stretch as much as the doughs made with just wheat flour.)

Use the pincer method to fully integrate the ingredients. Make five or six pincer cuts across the entire mass of dough. Then fold the dough over itself a few times. Repeat, alternately cutting and folding, until all the ingredients are fully integrated. Let the dough rest for a few minutes, then fold for another 30 seconds or until the dough tightens up. The whole process should take about 5 minutes. The target dough temperature at the end of the mix is 75° to 80°F / 24° to 27°C. Cover the tub and let the dough rise until the next fold.

3. Fold & First Rise

This dough needs three folds (see page 41). It's easiest to apply the folds during the first 1½ hours after mixing the dough. Apply the first fold about 10 minutes after mixing and the second and third when you see the dough spread out in the tub from the previous fold. If need be, it's okay to fold later; just be sure to leave it alone for the last hour of rising.

When the dough is about two and a half times its original volume, and the edge of the dough is about ½ inch below the 2-quart line in the dough tub, it's ready for you to make it into a loaf. If it is in a room at 70°F / 21°C, this first ferment should take 4 to 5 hours. It will happen faster in summer, so keep an eye on the volume expansion to make the call. Judge when it's ready based on volume expansion more than time. (If your kitchen is warmer or colder than mine, your time will vary.) If you're not using a marked dough tub, you'll have to eyeball it. Use your best judgment.

■ DAY 2, EVENING

4. Remove the Dough from Its Tub

Lightly flour a work surface about 12 inches wide. Flour your hands and sprinkle a bit of flour around the edges of the tub. Tip the tub slightly and gently work your floured free hand beneath the dough to loosen it from the bottom of the tub. Then turn the tub on its side and ease the dough out onto the work surface without pulling or tearing it.

5. Shape

Dust a proofing basket moderately with flour and spread the flour around with your hand. Shape the dough into a medium-tight ball following the instructions on pages 47 to 49. Place it seam-side down in its proofing basket.

6. Proof

Place the basket in a nonperforated plastic bag, tuck the bag under the basket, and refrigerate overnight.

The next morning, 12 to 16 hours after the loaf went into the refrigerator, it should be ready to bake, straight from the refrigerator. It does not need to come to room temperature first.

■ DAY 3, MORNING TO EARLY AFTERNOON

7. Preheat

About 45 minutes prior to baking, position a rack in the middle of the oven and put a Dutch oven, with its lid, on the rack. Preheat the oven to 475°F / 245°C.

8. Bake

For the next step, please be careful not to let your hands, fingers, or forearms touch the extremely hot Dutch oven.

Invert the basket with its proofed loaf onto a lightly floured countertop, keeping in mind that the top of the loaf will be the side that was facing down while it was rising—the seam side. Give the basket a firm tap on the countertop to pop the dough out.

Use oven mitts to remove the preheated Dutch oven from your oven, remove the lid, and carefully place the loaf, seam-side up, in the hot Dutch oven. Use the mitts to replace the lid, return the Dutch oven to the center of the middle rack, and bake for 30 minutes. Then carefully remove the lid and bake for about 20 minutes more, until dark brown all around the loaf. Check after 15 minutes of baking uncovered in case your oven runs hot.

Remove the Dutch oven and carefully tilt it to turn the loaf out. Let the loaf cool on a rack or set on its side, so air can circulate around it, for 20 minutes before slicing.

50% RYE BREAD
WITH WALNUTS

Dutch oven

You could make this without the walnuts, and the bread would be a sourdough version of the simpler same-day 50% Rye Bread on page 99. Both recipes make a hearty, European-style rye bread, though this one has much more flavor from the levain culture and the walnuts give it another dimension. I feel as though I should be somewhere else when I eat it, like in a rustic stone tavern in the Alps with fresh sheep's cheese and a cup of country red wine. Or you could have rye-walnut bread for breakfast in the suburbs with butter and honey. Food can make you travel without taking a step.

This bread is dense, a little smaller than the other loaves in this chapter, and delicious. It has a long shelf life when stored in an airtight bag or container. Slice it thinly, or at least not so thick that it's too chewy. It loves butter and cheese, but it's terrific just by itself. Have a toasted slice with a smear of fresh cheese and served with a salad. Wine and cold dark beer are happy companions too. Then, of course, if you pour some rye whiskey, you can have it two ways.

THIS RECIPE MAKES 1 DUTCH-OVEN LOAF OF ABOUT 2 POUNDS.

Please refer to the Seasonal Adjustments for Sourdough on page 187 for summer/winter changes.

First rise
About 5 hours at 70°F / 21°C room temperature,
maybe 4 hours in summer.

Proof time
Overnight in the refrigerator.

Bake
Preheat to 475°F / 245°C for 45 minutes,
bake at 475°F / 245°C about 50 minutes.

Sample schedule
Day 1, morning (*between 8 a.m. and noon*): Mix starter. Let sit out.

Day 1, evening (*8 to 12 hours later*): Second mix of starter. Let sit out.

Day 2, morning (*10 to 12 hours after previous night's mix*):
Mix starter again. Let sit out.

Day 2, afternoon (*7 to 8 hours after starter was mixed*): Final dough mix.
Give dough three folds. Rise time is about 4 hours in summer,
5 hours in winter.

Day 2, evening: Remove dough, shape loaf, let proof overnight
in refrigerator.

Day 3, morning: Bake.

STARTER: DAY 1, MORNING (between 8 a.m. and noon)

Ingredient	Quantity
Levain	50 to 60 g / ¼ cup
White bread flour	100 g / ½ cup + 3 Tbsp + 1¼ tsp
Water (75° to 80°F / 24° to 27°C; summer) (85°F / 29°C; winter)	100 g / ¼ cup + 2 Tbsp + 2 tsp

STARTER: DAY 1, EVENING (8 to 12 hours later)

Ingredient	Quantity
Morning starter mix	All of it
White bread flour	100 g / ½ cup + 3 Tbsp + 1¼ tsp
Water (70°F / 21°C; summer) (85°F / 29°C; winter)	100 g / ¼ cup + 2 Tbsp + 2 tsp

STARTER: DAY 2, MORNING (10 to 12 hours after previous night's mix)

Ingredient	Quantity
Starter	50 to 60 g / ¼ cup (summer) 75 g / ¼ cup + 2 Tbsp (winter)
White bread flour	100 g / ½ cup + 3 Tbsp + 1¼ tsp
Water (90° to 95°F / 32° to 35°C)	100 g / ¼ cup + 2 Tbsp + 2 tsp

FINAL DOUGH: DAY 2, AFTERNOON (7 to 8 hours after starter was mixed; 6 hours works if you keep the starter at 80° to 85°F / 27° to 29°C)

Ingredient	Quantity	Baker's Percentage
White bread flour*	150 g / 1 cup + 2 Tbsp + 2¼ tsp	50%
Whole or dark rye flour*	250 g / 1¾ cups + 2 Tbsp + 2¼ tsp	50%
Water (90° to 95°F / 32° to 35°C)	300 g / 1¼ cups	80%**
Fine sea salt	11 g / 2¼ tsp	2.2%
Starter*	200 g / 1 cup	20%
Walnut pieces (optional)	100 g / 1 cup	20%

*   Total flour includes flour in starter = 500 grams
** Includes water in starter

■ DAY 1, MORNING (between 8 a.m. and noon)

To begin the starter, weigh a 2-quart container with a lid (or a big bowl) while it's empty (without lid) and mark its weight on the container's side or write it down. You will need this info later.

Measure 100 grams (75° to 80°F / 24° to 27°C) water into your container. Add 50 to 60 grams levain from the refrigerator and stir a bit with your fingers to loosen up the culture. Add 100 grams white bread flour and mix with your fingers until all is incorporated.

Cover with the lid or plastic wrap and leave it out at room temperature. This works well at 70°F / 21°C room temperature. (If your kitchen is much warmer than that, e.g., 75° to 80°F / 24° to 27°C, use cooler water at 65° to 70°F / 18° to 21°C.) Put the levain back into the fridge.

■ DAY 1, EVENING (8 to 12 hours later)

Retain all the morning starter mix. Measure 100 grams (70°F / 21°C) water and 100 grams white bread flour into the same container on top of your first starter mix. Mix with your fingers until all is incorporated.

Cover with the lid or plastic wrap and leave it out at room temperature (65° to 70°F / 18° to 21°C) until the next morning. If it is summer and your kitchen is much warmer than that through the night, e.g., 75° to 80°F / 24° to 27°C, use cooler water again, this time about 60°F / 16°C. (Cooler than before because the rest of the starter is already at a warm room temperature. You don't want it to ferment too fast.)

▌ DAY 2, MORNING (10 to 12 hours after previous night's mix)

Around 8 a.m., reference the empty container weight and remove all but 50 to 60 grams of the Day 1 starter from your container. (Use the extra to make the excellent pizza dough on page 237, or toss it.) Measure 100 grams (95°F / 35°C) water into the container with the starter and mix with your fingers until you have a slurry. Add 100 grams white bread flour. Mix with your fingers until all is incorporated. Keep in a warm place, 70° to 75°F / 21° to 24°C.

▌ DAY 2, AFTERNOON (7 to 8 hours after starter was mixed)

Do a final dough mix using the following instructions. A visual cue that the starter is ready for this next phase is that at a certain point, there will be some small bubbles at the top. About an hour later, the whole top will be covered in little bubbles. It is at this second bubbly stage that the starter is ready. You will feel its light and gassy texture when you remove it to put it into your final dough mix. It will remain usable for a couple of hours before starting to develop more sour flavors.

1. Autolyse

Measure 300 grams (90° to 95°F / 32° to 35°C) water into a 6-quart round tub or similar container. Use a wet hand (so it doesn't stick) to add 200 grams of the Day 2 starter you mixed in the morning. Stir a bit with your fingers to loosen up the culture. Add 150 grams white bread flour and 250 grams whole or dark rye flour. Mix it by hand until all is incorporated.

Sprinkle 11 grams fine sea salt evenly across the top of the autolyse dough. Let it rest there, where it will partially dissolve.

Cover and let rest for 20 minutes. Measure out 100 grams walnut pieces so they will be on hand when you need them.

2. Mix

Because rye dough is sticky, you might want to use a flexible spatula or dough scraper to help unstick the dough from the bottom of the tub. It's good to dip the scraper into water first. Mix by hand, wetting your working hand before mixing so the dough doesn't stick to you. Reach underneath the dough and grab about one-fourth of it. Gently stretch this section and fold it over the top to the other side of the dough. Repeat three more times with the remaining dough until the salt is fully enclosed. (You'll notice the rye dough doesn't stretch as much as the doughs made with just wheat flour.)

Use the pincer method to fully integrate the ingredients. Make five or six pincer cuts across the entire mass of dough. Then fold the dough over itself a few times. Repeat, alternately cutting and folding, until all the ingredients are fully integrated. Add the 100 grams walnut pieces and use the same pincer method—cut and fold—to integrate the walnuts more or less evenly throughout the dough. Let the dough rest for a few minutes, then fold for another 30 seconds or until the dough tightens up. The whole process should take about 5 minutes. The target dough temperature at the end of the mix is 75° to 80°F / 23° to 26°C. Cover the tub and let the dough rise until the next fold.

3. Fold & First Rise

This dough needs three folds (see page 41). It's easiest to apply the folds during the first hour after mixing the dough. Apply the first fold about 10 minutes after mixing and the second and third when you see the dough spread out in the tub from the previous fold. If need be, it's okay to fold later; just be sure to leave it alone for the last hour of rising.

When the dough is about two and a half times its original volume, and the edge of the dough is about ½ inch below the 2-quart line in the dough tub, it's ready to be made up into a loaf. If it is in a room at 70°F / 21°C, this first ferment should take 4 to 5 hours. It will happen faster in summer, so keep an eye on the volume expansion to make the call. Judge when it's ready based on volume expansion more than time. (If your kitchen is warmer or colder than mine, your time will vary.) If you're not using a marked dough tub, you'll have to eyeball it. Use your best judgment.

■ DAY 2, EVENING

4. Remove the Dough from Its Tub

Lightly flour a work surface about 12 inches wide. Flour your hands and sprinkle a bit of flour around the edges of the tub. Tip the tub slightly and gently work your floured free hand beneath the dough to loosen it from the bottom of the tub. Then turn the tub on its side and ease the dough out onto the work surface without pulling or tearing it.

5. Shape

Rye bread benefits from a preshape, a 10-minute rest, and then a final shape before putting it into its proofing basket. This will build up the gluten strength and allow the best possible rise.

Dust a proofing basket moderately with flour and spread the flour around with your hand.

Holding part of the dough with one hand, use your other hand to stretch the dough out until it resists, then fold it back over itself. Turn and repeat over and over until you have formed a medium-tight round of dough. Cover and let rest for about 15 minutes.

Shape the dough again into a medium-tight ball. Place it seam-side down in its proofing basket.

6. Proof

Place the basket in a nonperforated plastic bag, tuck the bag under the basket, and refrigerate overnight.

The next morning, about 12 hours after the loaf went into the refrigerator, it should be ready to bake, straight from the refrigerator. It does not need to come to room temperature first.

■ DAY 3, MORNING

7. Preheat

About 45 minutes prior to baking, position a rack in the middle of the oven and put a Dutch oven, with its lid, on the rack. Preheat the oven to 475°F / 245°C.

8. Bake

For the next step, please be careful not to let your hands, fingers, or forearms touch the extremely hot Dutch oven.

Invert the basket with its proofed loaf onto a lightly floured countertop, keeping in mind that the top of the loaf will be the side that was facing down while it was rising—the seam side. Give the basket a firm tap on the countertop to pop the dough out.

Use oven mitts to remove the preheated Dutch oven from your oven, remove the lid, and carefully place the loaf, seam-side up, in the hot Dutch oven. Use the mitts to replace the lid, return the Dutch oven to the center of the middle rack, and bake for 30 minutes. Then carefully remove the lid and bake for about 20 minutes more, until dark brown all around the loaf. Check after 15 minutes of baking uncovered in case your oven runs hot.

Remove the Dutch oven and carefully tilt it to turn the loaf out. Let the loaf cool on a rack or set on its side, so air can circulate around it, for 1 hour before slicing.

APPLE-CIDER LEVAIN BREAD

Dutch oven

This is the apple bread we made in the early 2000s at Ken's Artisan Bakery. It was a hit at the farmers' market but tricky to bake because of the sugars that the cider added to the dough (if the oven was too hot, the loaves would scorch). Ultimately it fell out of our rotation. I made it again for a James Beard Foundation dinner in Portland in 2018, and it remains a personal favorite, even if we no longer make it at my bakery. I wrote this recipe as a Dutch-oven bread because that's a crustier loaf than the pan breads, and the flavor of the crust is fantastic.

Some unfiltered apple ciders, especially unpasteurized ones, will create a more actively fermented dough than filtered ciders. All will work, but the pace of the dough's rise will vary a little from one to the next. Nothing to worry about, but it's worth being aware of. You'll get a richer, more primal apple flavor from freshly pressed, unpasteurized cider. For a very different result, you could use sparkling cider. If your dough rises too fast, next time you can lower the temperature of the water in the final dough mix by about 10°F / 6°C to slow it down, or find a cooler place for it to ferment overnight.

Use whatever variety of apple you want. Core and chop the apple into small pieces (I like a small dice) to total between 75 and 100 grams.

If your oven, like most ovens, heats from the bottom, I advise setting up a heat shield (see page 52) halfway into the bake.

This bread tastes like an autumn day in the Shenandoah valley (cider country). It chars beautifully on the grill, on the stove top, or in a wood-fired oven and is great served with a spread of fresh veg, pâtés, meats, and cheeses.

THIS RECIPE MAKES 1 DUTCH-OVEN LOAF OF ABOUT 2⅓ POUNDS.

First rise
Overnight, 10 to 12 hours at room temperature
(65° to 70°F / 18° to 21°C). Faster if warmer, slower if cooler.
Cider speeds up the fermentation compared with water;
thus "cold" cider is used to compensate.

Proof time
3½ to 4 hours at 70°F / 21°C room temperature.

Bake
Preheat to 475°F / 245°C for 45 minutes,
bake at 475°F / 245°C for about 50 minutes.

Sample schedule
Day 1, evening: First mix of starter. Let sit out.

Day 2, morning (*12 to 15 hours later*): Mix starter again. Let sit out.

Day 2, evening (*10 to 12 hours after starter was mixed*): Final dough mix.
Give dough three folds. Rise time is overnight at room temperature.

Day 3, morning: Remove dough, shape loaf, let proof
at room temperature for about 3½ hours.

Day 3, afternoon: Bake.

STARTER: DAY 1, EVENING

Ingredient	Quantity
Levain	50 g / ¼ cup
White bread flour	100 g / ½ cup + 3 Tbsp + 1¼ tsp
Apple cider (cold)	100 g / ¼ cup + 2 Tbsp + 2 tsp

STARTER: DAY 2, MORNING (12 to 15 hours later)

Ingredient	Quantity
Day 1 starter	50 g / ¼ cup
White bread flour	100 g / ½ cup + 3 Tbsp + 1¼ tsp
Apple cider (cold)	100 g / ¼ cup + 2 Tbsp + 2 tsp

FINAL DOUGH: DAY 2, EVENING (10 to 12 hours after starter was mixed)

Ingredient	Quantity	Baker's Percentage
White bread flour*	264 g / 1¾ cups + 2 Tbsp + 2 tsp	60%
Whole-wheat flour*	110 g / ¾ cup + 1¾ tsp	20%
Whole or dark rye flour*	110 g / ¾ cup + 1 Tbsp + 1½ tsp	20%
Water (80°F / 27°C)	215 g / ¾ cup + 2 Tbsp + 1 tsp	39%
Apple cider (cold)	150 g / ½ cup + 2 Tbsp	39%**
Apple, in small dice (optional)	75 to 100 g (1 small apple)	15 to 20%
Fine sea salt	12 g / scant 2½ tsp	2.2%
Starter*	132 g / ⅔ cup	12%

* Total flour includes flour in starter = 550 grams

** Includes cider in starter

To begin the starter, weigh a 2-quart container with a lid (or a big bowl) while it's empty (without lid) and mark its weight on the container's side or write it down. You will need this info later.

Measure 100 grams cold apple cider into your container. Add 50 grams levain from the refrigerator and stir a bit with your fingers to loosen up the culture. Add 100 grams white bread flour and mix by hand until all is incorporated.

Cover with the lid or plastic wrap and leave it out at room temperature until the next morning. This works well at room temperature (65° to 70°F / 18° to 21°C). If it is summer and your kitchen is much warmer than that through the night, please wait until 8 p.m. or 9 p.m. to feed the starter.

Keep the cider in the fridge.

■ DAY 2, MORNING (12 to 15 hours later)

First thing in the morning, reference the empty container weight and remove all but 50 grams of the Day 1 starter from your container. (Use the extra to make pancakes—hold in the refrigerator and just blend it in to a pancake batter you already use—or toss it.) Measure 100 grams cold apple cider into the container with the starter and mix with your fingers until you have a slurry (refrigerate the cider for the evening's final dough mix). Add 100 grams white bread flour. Mix with your fingers until all is incorporated. Keep in a warm place, 70° to 75°F / 21° to 24°C.

■ DAY 2, EVENING (10 to 12 hours after starter was mixed)

Chop a small apple, skin on, into half-dime-size or smaller pieces and set aside. You can cut around the core, then chop, rinse in cold water, and drain the chopped pieces.

Do a final dough mix using the following instructions.

1. Autolyse

Measure 215 grams (80°F / 26°C) water into a 6-quart round tub or similar container. Add 150 grams cold apple cider. Use a wet hand (so it doesn't stick) to add 132 grams (it's fine to be a little above, up to 150 grams) of the starter you mixed in the morning (it will be funky!). Stir a bit with your fingers to loosen up the culture. Add 264 grams white bread flour, 110 grams whole-wheat flour, 110 grams rye flour, and chopped apples. Mix it by hand until all is incorporated.

Sprinkle 12 grams fine sea salt evenly across the top of the autolyse dough. Let it rest there, where it will partially dissolve.

Cover and let rest for 20 minutes.

2. Mix

Mix by hand, wetting your working hand before mixing so the dough doesn't stick to you. Reach underneath the dough and grab about one-fourth of it. Gently stretch this section and fold it over the top to the other side of the dough. Repeat three more times with the remaining dough until the salt is fully enclosed. (You'll notice the rye dough doesn't stretch as much as the doughs made with just wheat flour.)

Use the pincer method to fully integrate the ingredients. Make five or six pincer cuts across the entire mass of dough. Then fold the dough over itself a few times. Repeat, alternately cutting and folding, until all the ingredients are fully integrated. Let the dough rest for a couple minutes, then fold for another 30 seconds or until the dough tightens up. The whole process should take about 5 minutes. The target dough temperature at the end of the mix is about 65°F / 18°C. Cover the tub and let the dough rise until the next fold.

3. Fold & First Rise

This dough needs two folds (see page 41). It's easiest to apply the folds during the first 1½ hours after mixing the dough. Apply the first fold about 10 minutes after mixing and the second when you see the dough spread out in the tub. Leave it out overnight in a spot that is 65° to 70°F / 18° to 21°C. In my test bakes, the dough rising overnight at 65°F / 18°C was ready in 11 hours.

■ DAY 3, MORNING

When the dough is nearly three times its original volume, or the edge of the dough is all the way up to the 2-quart line in the dough tub, it's ready to be made up into a loaf. The dough should be domed— not flattened, not collapsed. (If it's well above the 2-quart line, it has risen too much but keep going!— mix with cooler water next time or find a cooler place for it overnight.) If you're not using a marked dough tub, you'll have to eyeball it. Use your best judgment.

4. Remove the Dough from Its Tub

Lightly flour a work surface about 12 inches wide. Flour your hands and sprinkle a bit of flour around the edges of the tub. Tip the tub slightly and gently work your floured free hand beneath the dough to loosen it from the bottom of the tub. Then turn the tub on its side and ease the dough out onto the work surface without pulling or tearing it.

5. Shape

Dust a proofing basket moderately with flour and spread the flour around with your hand. Shape the dough into a medium-tight ball following the instructions on pages 47 to 49. Place it seam-side down in its proofing basket.

6. Proof

Place the basket in a nonperforated plastic bag, tuck the bag under the basket, and leave it out at room temperature. Proofing time should be about 3½ hours, assuming a room temperature of about 70°F / 21°C.

Use the refrigerator if you need to extend the proof time. Refrigerate the covered loaf about 2 hours into the proof period and bake 4 to 6 hours later. It does not need to come to room temperature before baking.

7. Preheat

About 45 minutes prior to baking, position a rack in the middle of the oven and put a Dutch oven, with its lid, on the rack. Preheat the oven to 475°F / 245°C.

8. Bake

For the next step, please be careful not to let your hands, fingers, or forearms touch the extremely hot Dutch oven.

Invert the basket with its proofed loaf onto a lightly floured countertop, keeping in mind that the top of the loaf will be the side that was facing down while it was rising—the seam side. Give the basket a firm tap on the countertop to pop the dough out.

Use oven mitts to remove the preheated Dutch oven from your oven, take off the lid, and carefully place the loaf, seam-side up, in the hot Dutch oven. Use the mitts to replace the lid, return the Dutch oven to the center of the middle rack, and bake for 30 minutes, then slide a heat shield onto the rack below the Dutch oven. Carefully remove the lid and bake for about 20 minutes more, until dark brown all around the loaf. Check after 15 minutes of baking uncovered in case your oven runs hot, and then stay with it, checking frequently for the final 5 minutes of the bake. Go dark, but be careful not to let it burn.

If you want, near the end of your bake, it's fine to pull the Dutch oven out of the oven, remove the loaf, and examine on all sides for color. Then you have a point of reference for how you want to finish the bake, in or out of the Dutch oven. You could place the nearly done loaf directly on the oven rack the last few minutes of baking, which will make it crustier than if it finishes in the Dutch oven.

Let the loaf cool on a rack or set on its side, so air can circulate around it, for 30 minutes before slicing.

Apple-Cider Bread Schedule

Timing is everything in breadland! Each stage in this Apple-Cider Levain Bread recipe has a need for the dough to ferment enough to provide a good amount of leavening power in the next step but not so much that the bread turns sour. You can trust my timing and temperature combinations; they have been tested over and over. In this recipe, the time you mix the Day 1 starter will determine the timing of every future step in the recipe, including when you bake the bread. If you begin with the mix of the Day 1 starter at 6 p.m. or 7 p.m., the rest of the schedule will flow on a timeline that I think will work for a lot of people with a fairly normal sleep schedule. If you work overnight, or the schedule outlined here doesn't work for you, you can adjust based on the elapsed timelines that I list in each step. Happy baking!

PIZZA DOUGH FROM "EXTRA" LEVAIN STARTER

As explained in chapter 3, making more levain culture than you need is often a necessary part of sourdough baking when the recipe is for one or two loaves. (This is a small-batch problem. Large batches can build up without any waste.) The extra starter comes from the need to create enough leavening power in the culture and to build a balance of flavors. There are many options for making up something else from the extra starter, such as pancakes and muffins. Pizza dough is my favorite choice, and you can make this up quickly and easily. The ingredients are the same as for bread dough and you will already have everything you need at hand. You can make pizza for lunch the next day, that night, or up to two nights later.

In this book's Dutch-oven levain bread process, I have you make up a starter from a refrigerated levain. The final starter feeding on Day 2 has you remove about 400 grams of starter (leaving behind 50 to 60 grams for the buildup for the final dough mix). So, let's make pizza dough with that extra starter. There will be zero waste and a very good dough that will give you puffy rims and an assertive sourdough flavor. I like it, and I also like the zero waste; but it might be too much for some, so I have a second recipe table with ingredient amounts for a mellower-flavored sourdough pizza dough.

You will be using the Day 2 starter as your levain for this pizza dough, and that starter gets mixed in the morning. If you want pizza that night and are mixing the dough in the morning, you will want to refrigerate the dough balls in the mid-afternoon for a couple hours and then pull them from the refrigerator to warm back up an hour or so before you make pizza.

THIS RECIPE MAKES 823 GRAMS OF PIZZA DOUGH,
ENOUGH FOR 3 TWELVE-INCH PIZZAS OR 1 PAN PIZZA.

First rise
1 hour.

Proof time
4 to 5 hours at 70°F / 21°C room temperature, or refrigerate
after 3 hours to make pizza within the next 2 days.

Ingredient	Quantity	Baker's Percentage
White bread or pizza flour*	300 g / 2 cups + 2 Tbsp + 1¼ tsp	100%
Water (80°F / 27°C)	140 g / ½ cup + 2 Tbsp	67%**
Fine sea salt	13 g / 2½ tsp	2.7%
Starter*	370 g / 1¾ cups + 1 tbsp	38%

* Total flour includes flour in starter = 485 grams

** Includes water in starter

1. Mix the Dough

Measure 140 grams (80°F / 27°C) water into a 6-quart dough tub or a large mixing bowl. Add 13 grams fine sea salt and swish around until the salt is dissolved.

Add all 370 grams starter. (The math says your extra starter should weigh 400 grams, but there's always some that sticks to its container or to the baker's hand. Don't sweat it. Approximate amounts here are fine.) Mix thoroughly with your hand until the starter and water are completely blended.

Add 200 grams of the flour and mix by hand. Once the loose flour is integrated and you have formed a mass of dough, add the remaining 100 grams flour and complete the mix.

Use the pincer method to mix as for the bread doughs and completely integrate the loose flour into the dough. This pizza dough is stiffer than my bread doughs, and you will need to work a little harder to mix this by hand, but it's easier if you add the flour in two stages than if you add it all at once.

Cover and let rest for 10 minutes. Then fold the dough over itself a few times until you have formed a cohesive round of dough. Cover and let rest for 1 hour.

2. Divide and Make Up Dough Balls

Divide the dough into three equal portions and shape each into a round ball, or shape the dough into a single large dough ball for pan pizza. Place the dough on a large plate or a small baking sheet and cover with plastic wrap to prevent the dough from drying out.

3. Dough Ball Rise

Let the dough sit out for 4 to 5 hours at room temperature and then use to make pizza anytime in the following 2 hours. Or refrigerate after 3 hours and make pizza later that day or sometime within the next 2 days. Be sure to take the dough balls out of the refrigerator 1 to 2 hours before making pizza. Then it will stretch out real easy.

MELLOW SOURDOUGH PIZZA DOUGH

Instead of using the full amount of leftover starter, this option incorporates just 200 grams.

Ingredient	Quantity	Baker's Percentage
White bread flour*	400 g / 2¾ cups + 2 tsp	100%
Water (80°F / 27°C)	235 g / 1 cup	67%**
Fine sea salt	13 g / 2½ tsp	2.6%
Starter*	200 g / 1 cup	20%

* Total flour includes flour in the starter = 500 grams
** Includes water in starter

Follow the main recipe instructions.

ACKNOWLEDGMENTS

I have to pay tribute to the irreplaceable work of Kat Merck, who has done first line editing and recipe testing for all three of my books. The steady email dialog that we had, morning and night, was fun in itself, and for this book her work was essential. Kat tested every recipe in this book and fed her family a lot of bread. Her input and her sharing of successes and not-so-much-successes helped me refine the recipes to work for you.

I am proud to be an author for Ten Speed Press. A big shout-out to Kelly Snowden, who was the editor for this book, and the supporting cast who made it look like I can pass an English composition class. Also, a special tip of the hat to Betsy Stromberg, who did the design and layout of this beautiful book.

Finally, Alan Weiner has photographed all three of my books. Alan worked as a photojournalist for the *New York Times* for over twenty years, and I knew from the beginning that his eye for the interesting detail would suit my photographic taste in cookbook production. When I got my first copy of this book, with photos placed throughout, I was thrilled, and when I flip through it, I admire the photography every time.

ABOUT THE CONTRIBUTORS

KEN FORKISH is the founder of Ken's Artisan Bakery, Ken's Artisan Pizza, and Checkerboard Pizza, all in Portland, Oregon. He is also the author of James Beard Award– and IACP Award–winning book *Flour Water Salt Yeast* and a 2016 ode to pizza, *The Elements of Pizza*.

Ken was a key contributor to Portland's culinary evolution, founding Ken's Artisan Bakery in 2001 and Ken's Artisan Pizza in 2006. He was a finalist for the national James Beard Award for Outstanding Pastry Chef in 2013 and Outstanding Baker in 2017. In 2013, Ken opened Trifecta Tavern & Bakery, an award-winning bar, restaurant, and small-batch bakery that closed at its peak in late 2019. Ken's Artisan Bakery was sold to two long-standing employees, and Ken's Artisan Pizza was sold to a longtime friend.

His expert recipe tester for the book was Junior (pictured below).

ALAN WEINER fell hopelessly in love with photography when he was ten years old. After earning a degree in journalism, he worked for the *New York Times*, traveling the world for twenty years. Since then, he has worked as a food, portrait, and corporate photographer. He is based in Portland, Oregon.

Junior

INDEX

Ten Speed Press and the Ten Speed Press colophon are registered
trademarks of Penguin Random House LLC.

Typefaces: Hoefler & Frere-Jones's Chronicle Text, Joshua Darden's Freight
Sans, and Andrew Paglinawan's Quicksand

Image on page 9 by Tefi/Shutterstock.com

Library of Congress Control Number: 2022936137

Hardcover ISBN: 978-1-9848-6037-8
eBook ISBN: 978-1-9848-6038-5

Printed in China

Editor: Kelly Snowden
Production editor: Sohayla Farman
Designer: Betsy Stromberg | Production designers: Mari Gill and Faith Hague
Production manager: Jane Chinn | Prepress color manager: Nick Patton
Copyeditor: Sharon Silva | Proofreader: Elisabeth Beller
Indexer: Elizabeth Parson
Publicist: Kristin Casemore | Marketers: Chloe Aryeh and Windy Dorresteyn

10 9 8 7 6 5 4 3 2 1

First Edition